BARBECUES

BARBECUES

Over 200 great recipes

hamlyn

An Hachette Livre UK Company
www.hachettelivre.co.uk

First published in Great Britain in 2008 by Hamlyn,
a division of Octopus Publishing Group Ltd
2–4 Heron Quays, London E14 4JP

www.octopusbooks.co.uk

Copyright © Octopus Publishing Group Ltd 2008

ISBN 978-0-600-61792-1

A CIP catalogue record for this book is available from the British
Library

Printed and bound in China

10 9 8 7 6 5 4 3 2 1

Notes

This book includes dishes made with nuts and nut derivatives. It
is advisable for those with known allergic reactions to nuts and
nut derivatives and those who may be potentially vulnerable to
these allergies, such as pregnant and nursing mothers, invalids,
the elderly, babies and children, to avoid dishes made with nuts
and nut oils. It is also prudent to check the labels of preprepared
ingredients for the possible inclusion of nut derivatives.

Both metric and imperial measurements are given for the
recipes. Use one set of measures only, not a mixture of both.

Fresh herbs should be used unless otherwise stated.

Figures given for preparation and cooking times ('Prep' and
'Cook') are given in minutes.

All cooking times are approximate as cooking times may be
affected by such factors as altitude, wind, outside temperature
and desired doneness.

contents

Introduction

There's nothing quite like a barbecue. The preparation; the anticipation of waiting for the coals to heat up; the mouth-watering smells; and the delicious, woody flavour of freshly cooked food make this a popular meal option for warm summer days. However, advances in barbecue technology and the rather unreliable nature of the British summer have meant that barbecuing is no longer confined to those few short weeks when the sun makes an appearance. Indeed, just the thought of a barbecue can lift the spirits and create an instant holiday atmosphere so, as long as you have a bit of shelter to do the actual cooking, you can barbecue whatever the weather.

Be prepared

Many people have a barbecue tucked away in a corner of their garden and often it will remain hidden under a cover from one year to the next. It can sometimes seem like a bit of an effort to clean it off and light it up, especially if you are planning an impromptu gathering. If you get used to using the barbecue all year round and make a point of cleaning the grill and bowl after each use then it will always be ready to fire up at a moment's notice. It is also a good idea to keep a ready supply of charcoal, matches, skewers etc at home as it is not always possible to get hold of barbecue equipment out of season. That way, if you have the urge to barbecue, or there is a spell of hot weather later on in the year, you can make the most of it!

Recipe for success

Over the following pages you will discover recipes for all tastes and occasions, as well as marinades, dips and sauces to accompany them. There are classic meat dishes such as The Ultimate Cheeseburger (page 24), and Veal Escalopes with Artichoke Paste (page 58), as well as more unusual fish and shellfish recipes like Whole Baked Fish in Banana Leaves (page 110) and Spicy Fish Satay (page 105). There are also chapters dedicated to vegetarian recipes; and salads, desserts and accompaniments. So, whether you are looking for ideas for speedy suppers or something more adventurous for entertaining, you will find everything you need here.

Your barbecue

Before you buy a barbecue you need to think about a number of factors, such as the amount you are going to use it. If you plan on barbecuing all year round then it is probably worth spending a bit more and you might opt for the convenience of a gas model. They are quick and easy to use and you don't need to worry about running out of charcoal before the burgers have cooked through. Gas models usually have built-in work surfaces and sturdy covers, making them even more convenient. The only downside is that they tend to be bigger than other styles so this is only really an option if you have a decent-sized garden.

If you have a smaller outside space, a more compact kettle barbecue is probably a better choice. They are generally a simple round bowl with a lid and a grill rack that has an adjustable height so you can control the cooking times and temperature to some extent. Another option is to have a built-in barbecue. This can work for gardens of any size as you can design the barbecue to fit the desired space and you can also create storage areas and work surfaces. If space is extremely tight but you don't want to miss out on those summer al fresco meals, then you can always buy disposable barbecues as and when you need them. They tend to be very basic and quite small but they do the job and can produce pretty good results.

If you look after your barbecue it should give you many years of service. It is obviously important to keep it dry so, if you have a shed or other sheltered area, store it there when not in use. Alternatively, it is possible to buy a special waterproof cover that should keep it protected from the elements. You should also make sure you store the charcoal somewhere dry.

How to barbecue

Despite the stereotypical image of a group of hungry guests standing idly around as the host battles with lukewarm coals and a rack of anaemic-looking sausages barbecuing is actually an easy and relaxed way to cook. Although there is a bit of a knack to getting the coals to reach exactly the right temperature for cooking, once you've mastered the technique you can just light them up then sit back with a cold drink and wait until the barbecue is hot enough for cooking.

1 Get organized at least 30 minutes before you want to eat and start by lining the tray with kitchen foil (this makes it easier to clean afterwards).

2 Dot some firelighters (or newspaper) amongst the charcoal and build it up to a cone shape in the middle of the tray so that the fire takes more easily. Light the coals and leave alone until they have burnt down to embers. This is the key – don't be tempted to start cooking before the coals are hot enough!

3 Spread the embers evenly over the tray and brush the grill with a little oil so the food doesn't stick to it.

4 If you need to add more coals to keep the barbecue going, place them around the edges and then gradually move them to the centre as they heat up.

Barbecue food

While sausages and burgers are generally seen as staple barbecue fodder, it is actually possible to cook almost any type of food on a barbecue. If you enjoy the rich, smoky flavour that the coals impart to food then why not get creative and try some of the more unusual recipes in this book? The more adventurous you are, the more unlikely it is that your shiny new barbecue will be left languishing in a corner for most of the year.

✳ Meat

Meat is definitely the most barbecued foodstuff and probably with good reason. Most varieties and cuts of meat take well to being cooked over hot coals and the robust nature of steaks, sausages and ribs mean they remain intact even after a rigorous attack with prongs by over-eager chefs. Steak is a popular choice and a well-prepared barbecue will do justice to a really nice steak. The key is not to overcomplicate it with too many flavourings: just let the quality of the meat and the natural flavours of the smoke do the work. If your coals are hot, a steak can be cooked in minutes, so it is also a good option for cooking first and keeping hungry guests satisfied.

Sausages and burgers are a must for any barbecue and are a particularly good choice for kids as they can make up their own hot dogs or burgers with garnishes and sauces. Keep it classic or try something a little more adventurous, such as Greek-Style Lamb Burgers (page 38). Homemade burgers can be prepared in advance and kept in the refrigerator until you are ready to start cooking, as can dips and sauces, so you won't need to spend hours in the kitchen once your guests arrive.

❋ Poultry

All types of poultry work really well on the barbecue, as the meat remains juicy and tender while absorbing all the wonderful smoky flavours. Cuts with the bone left in are a good choice because the bone will help keep the meat moist as it cooks. A simple oil and citrus marinade will add extra flavour and the meat can be marinated in the refrigerator for a couple of hours before cooking. Chicken, in particular, is also great for kebabs and brochettes: try the delicious Chicken Satay recipe on page 75. Smaller pieces of chicken mean a quick cooking time so these would be ideal for a starter.

❋ Fish

Fish is an underrated barbecue food and yet it is perfect for al fresco dining. If you are cooking straight on the grill it is best to choose a meaty, robust fish, such as monkfish or swordfish. Alternatively, you can cook whole fish in specially designed fish racks or wrap whole fish, fish fillets or shellfish in foil with a little oil, garlic and some herbs and then steam on the grill. Fish combines well with all manner of marinades and you'll find plenty of delicious recipes in the fish chapter such as Mussels and Clams Marinière (page 133).

❋ Vegetarian dishes

Vegetarians don't need to miss out just because the barbecue is being lit up. There are plenty of options for delicious vegetarian dishes. If you are cooking meat and vegetarian food on the same grill make sure you keep them to separate areas and use different utensils and dishes to handle and store the food. Veggie burgers such as Falafel Burgers (page 136) make a good alternative to main meat dishes, while sides such as Stuffed Mini Peppers with Tomato Sauce (page 145) will be eagerly devoured by both vegetarians and meat eaters alike. Whether it's whole barbecued vegetables, kebabs or steamed parcels, there are plenty of creative ideas for meat-free barbecue dishes.

Simple barbecuing

✳ Equipment

Although not absolutely essential, the following items will make for easier barbecuing.

Long-handled tongs: Useful for turning food and putting it on and taking it off the grill. Use a separate pair for the coals.

Long-pronged fork: Don't pierce food while it is cooking; this will remove precious juices and flavours and dry out the food. Use the fork only towards the end of cooking to check if meat or poultry is cooked.

Skewers: For brochettes and kebabs – soak wooden skewers for 30 minutes before use to prevent burning.

Drip Tray: Heavy-duty foil or a metal freezer tray can be placed under the food to catch the juices for basting or for use in the finished sauce. It also prevents flare-ups from dripping fat.

✳ Cooking on the barbecue

1 Make sure that you have sufficient fuel for your barbecue.

2 Always oil the barbecue grill well to prevent food from sticking.

3 Wear an apron to protect your clothes and oven gloves to protect your hands from being burnt.

4 Go easy on the salt in marinades for meat as salt draws out the juices and dries the meat. Season just before or just after cooking.

5 Keep food in the refrigerator before use and bring it to room temperature just before cooking.

6 Cut food to an even size so it will cook evenly. Place longer-cooking foods on the barbecue first, then add any quick-cooking items.

7 Remember that food continues to cook after you remove it from the heat.

8 Never use petrol, paraffin or other flammable liquids when lighting your fire. Be safe!

General techniques

✳ Spatchcocking

Spatchcocking is used for small and medium birds, such as poussin, small chickens, pheasant, quail or guinea fowl so that they lie flat and can be grilled, barbecued or roasted quickly and evenly. Spatchcocked birds can be marinated or flavoured with herbs and spices before they are cooked.

1 With the bird breast side down, use strong poultry shears to cut through the flesh and ribs to one side of the backbone. Cut down the other side of the backbone, then discard it. Remove the small wishbone at the neck end.

2 Turn the bird over, breast side up. To open out and flatten the bird, press firmly on the breastbone with the heel of your hand.

3 To keep the bird flat and easy to turn during cooking, thread two wooden or metal skewers diagonally across through the bird. Push the first through a wing on one side and out through the thickest part of the thigh on the other side. Push the second skewer through parallel to the first towards the other end of the bird.

✳ Skinning tomatoes

There are two simple ways to skin tomatoes. The first is to drop them whole into a bowl of boiling water and leave for 1 minute. Then lift them out with a slotted spoon and drop them into a bowl of cold water. Slit the skins and peel. Alternatively, spear a tomato firmly on a fork, then hold it in the flame of a gas hob. Turn the tomato evenly until the skin blisters and splits, and peel.

✳ Skinning peppers

The easiest way to remove the skins from peppers is to grill them until blistered and charred. This also tenderizes the flesh and improves its flavour. Preheat the grill on the hottest setting, cut the peppers in half and remove the seeds and core. Then place the peppers cut side down on a foil-lined grill pan and place under the hot grill. Cook until the skins are blackened and split, then remove from the heat and place the peppers in a plastic bag. Leave them until cool enough to handle, when the skins will peel easily.

meat

1 kg (2 lb) good-quality coarsely minced **beef**

2 **garlic cloves**, crushed

8 **streaky bacon** rashers

a little light **olive oil**, for brushing

salt and **pepper**

TO SERVE

4 large **burger buns**

75 g (3 oz) mixed **salad leaves**

1 **beef tomato**, sliced

4 thick slices of strong **Cheddar cheese** or **Monterey Jack**

1 small **red onion**, sliced into rings

1 quantity **Quick BBQ Sauce** (see page 230)

PREP
15*

COOK
15

SERVES
4

hearty

Classic American burgers

This one is for adults only; with a full 250 g (8 oz) of burger per person, it makes a hearty meal for every real meat lover.

1 Mix the beef and garlic and season well with salt and pepper. Divide the mixture into 4 portions and shape each one into a ball, then flatten slightly into burgers. Cover and chill for 30 minutes.

2 Grill the bacon until slightly crisp and keep it warm. Brush the burgers with a little oil and cook them on an oiled barbecue grill over medium-hot coals for 5–6 minutes on each side, depending on how you like them cooked.

3 To assemble, cover the base of each bun first with salad leaves, then tomato slices. Place the cooked burger on the salad then top with the cheese, bacon and a little sliced red onion. Serve open or topped with the bun lid and accompanied with lots of quick BBQ sauce.

* plus 30 minutes chilling

Chorizo burgers with red wine jus

You can buy chargrilled peppers preserved in jars to save time. If you want to make your own, simply char the skin of a pepper under a grill until black, then peel off the blackened skin.

1 Mix the beef with the chorizo, red pepper, parsley and paprika and season well with salt and pepper. Divide the mixture into 4 portions and shape each one into a ball, then flatten slightly into a burger. Cover and chill for 30 minutes.

2 Brush the burgers with a little oil and cook them on an oiled barbecue grill over medium-hot coals for 5–6 minutes on each side, depending on how you like them cooked. Meanwhile, heat the oil in a frying pan and fry the onions and garlic until softened, about 2 minutes. Next, add the sugar and red wine and simmer until the liquid has reduced and the sauce is slightly sticky.

3 To assemble, halve and toast the rolls on the barbecue, add the rocket then the burgers, spoon over the red wine jus and serve.

PREP
20*

COOK
15

SERVES
4

spicy

500 g (1 lb) good-quality coarsely minced **beef**

250 g (8 oz) spicy **chorizo sausage**, skinned and finely chopped

125 g (4 oz) **chargrilled red peppers**, finely chopped

2 tablespoons chopped **flat leaf parsley**

1 teaspoon **smoked paprika**

2 tablespoons light **olive oil**

½ **red onion**, finely chopped

1 **garlic clove**, crushed

1 teaspoon **sugar**

125 ml (4 fl oz) **red wine**

salt and **pepper**

TO SERVE

4 **sesame seed rolls**

75 g (3 oz) **rocket**

1 tablespoon light **olive oil**, plus extra for brushing

1 **red onion**, finely chopped

3 **garlic cloves**

625 g (1¼ lb) good-quality coarsely minced **beef**

2 tablespoons chopped **basil**

2 tablespoons chopped **marjoram**

2 tablespoons chopped **oregano**

50 g (2 oz) freshly grated **Parmesan cheese**

75 g (3 oz) **sun-dried tomatoes**, finely chopped

75 g (3 oz) **black olives**, finely chopped

salt and **pepper**

TO SERVE

2 **focaccia rolls**, quartered

1 quantity **Basil Mayonnaise** (see page 237)

75 g (3 oz) **rocket**

1 ball of **mozzarella cheese**, about 125 g (4 oz), torn into pieces

1 small bunch of **basil**

PREP
20*

COOK
15

SERVES
4

rustic

Sicilian burgers

These rustic, herby burgers have the taste of Italy: tomatoes, olives and oregano.

1 Heat the oil in a frying pan and fry the onion and garlic over a medium heat for 4 minutes or until softened. Set aside to cool. Put the beef, onion and garlic mixture, herbs, Parmesan, tomatoes and olives in a large bowl. Season with salt and pepper and mix well. Divide the mixture into 8 portions and shape each one into a ball, then flatten slightly into a burger. Cover and chill for 30 minutes.

2 Brush the burgers with a little oil and cook them on an oiled barbecue grill over medium-hot coals for 4–5 minutes on each side until slightly charred on the outside and medium rare in the centre.

3 To assemble, split the quartered focaccia rolls in half and toast lightly on the barbecue. Spread the bases with basil mayonnaise and top with rocket and the cooked burgers. Divide the mozzarella pieces among the 8 burgers. Top with the lids and a basil leaf and secure with a cocktail stick. Serve with extra basil mayonnaise and rocket.

* plus 30 minutes chilling

Mexico City burgers with avocado salsa

The taco seasoning, jalapeño peppers and Tabasco sauce make sure these burgers are a sure winner, and using tortilla wraps instead of burger buns makes for a welcome change.

1 Heat the oil in a frying pan and cook the onion with the taco seasoning for about 3–4 minutes until soft. Leave to cool, then season with salt and pepper and mix with the beef, coriander, jalapeño peppers and Tabasco sauce. Divide the mixture into 8 portions, shape each one into a ball, then flatten slightly. Cover and chill for at least 30 minutes.

2 Meanwhile, combine all the ingredients for the salsa in a small bowl. Chill to allow the flavours to develop.

3 Brush the burgers with a little oil and cook them on an oiled barbecue grill over medium-hot coals for 5–6 minutes on each side, depending on how you like them cooked.

4 To assemble, warm the soft tortillas under a grill. Place some of the lettuce over each tortilla then add two of the mini burgers. Top with a few spoonfuls of salsa and a dollop of soured cream. Fold the tortillas in half and serve.

PREP
20*

COOK
20

SERVES
4

fiery

1 tablespoon light **olive oil**, plus extra for brushing

1 **onion**, finely chopped

2½ tablespoons **taco seasoning**

625 g (1¼ lb) good-quality coarsely minced **beef**

2 tablespoons chopped **coriander**

25 g (1 oz) **jalapeño peppers**

1 teaspoon **Tabasco sauce**

salt and **pepper**

AVOCADO SALSA

1 **avocado**, peeled and diced

2 large **tomatoes**, skinned (see page 13), deseeded and diced

1 **red chilli**, deseeded and finely chopped

4 **spring onions**, thinly shredded

2 tablespoons chopped **coriander**

juice and grated rind of 1 **lime**

3 tablespoons **olive oil**

TO SERVE

4 **soft tortillas**

iceberg lettuce, shredded

50 ml (2 fl oz) **soured cream**

625 g (1¼ lb) good-quality coarsely minced **beef**

1 small **red onion**, finely chopped

2 **garlic cloves**, crushed

2 teaspoons **dried basil**

1 ball of **mozzarella cheese** or 4 **bocconcini**

4 thin slices of **prosciutto**

a little light **olive oil**, for brushing

salt and **pepper**

PESTO

25 g (1 oz) **basil**, chopped

25 g (1 oz) **Parmesan cheese**, grated

1 **garlic clove**, crushed

25 g (1 oz) **pine nuts**, roasted

75 ml (3 fl oz) **olive oil**

salt and **pepper**

TO SERVE:

8 slices of **sourdough bread** (see page 206)

2 **tomatoes**, sliced

50 g (2 oz) **rocket**

PREP
30*

COOK
12

SERVES
4

Italian

Pesto burgers

Homemade pesto is better than shop-bought. If you need to buy it, get it fresh, from an Italian delicatessen. If you make your own, you can roast the pine nuts in a pan or buy them ready-roasted.

1 To make the pesto sauce, put all the ingredients in a food processor and process until the mixture resembles a smooth sauce. Season to taste with salt and pepper, adding a little more oil if necessary.

2 Mix together the beef, onion, garlic and basil in a bowl and season well with salt and pepper. Divide the mixture into 4 portions. Form them into balls around a piece of mozzarella or a bocconcini, then wrap each burger in a slice of prosciutto. Cover and chill for 1 hour.

3 Brush the burgers with a little oil and cook them on an oiled barbecue grill over medium-hot coals for 5–6 minutes on each side, depending on how you like them cooked.

4 To assemble, spread the slices of bread with a little pesto and toast on the barbecue until golden. Top each slice with a few slices of tomato, some rocket and a burger. Drizzle each with a little pesto and serve with the remaining slices of bread.

* plus 1 hour chilling

Blue-cheese burgers

The strong flavours of this tasty burger – mustard and blue cheese – are softened by the unusual addition of some pear, which also adds moistness.

1 Heat the oil in a frying pan and cook the onion and garlic over a medium heat for about 5 minutes or until softened. Set aside to cool. Mix together the minced beef, the onion and garlic mixture, chives, pear and mustard. Season well with salt and pepper. Divide the mixture into 4 portions and shape each one into a ball, then flatten slightly into a burger. Cover and chill for 30 minutes.

2 Melt the butter in a small pan and add the mushrooms. Fry for about 5 minutes, then set aside to cool. Brush the burgers with a little oil and cook them on an oiled barbecue grill over medium-hot coals for 5–6 minutes on each side, depending on how you like them cooked. Divide the blue cheese into 4 portions, place one on the top of each burger then allow the cheese to melt slightly in the heat from the barbecue.

3 To assemble, toast the slices of walnut bread on the barbecue until lightly browned. Top each slice with some of the fried mushrooms and a burger. Garnish with the watercress and chopped chives and serve immediately.

PREP
20*

COOK
20

SERVES
4

tasty

1 tablespoon **vegetable oil**

1 **onion**, finely chopped

2 **garlic cloves**, crushed

625 g (1¼ lb) good-quality coarsely minced **beef**

2 tablespoons finely chopped **chives**

1 **pear**, peeled, cored and grated

1 tablespoon **wholegrain mustard**

25 g (1 oz) **butter**

3 **field mushrooms**, thickly sliced

a little light **olive oil**, for brushing

150 g (5 oz) **blue cheese**

salt and **pepper**

TO SERVE

4 thick slices of **walnut bread**

1 bunch of **watercress**

a few chopped **chives**

75 g (3 oz) **butter**

3 **garlic cloves**, crushed

2 tablespoons chopped **parsley**

650 g (1 lb 5 oz) good-quality coarsely minced **beef**

100 g (3½ oz) **sun-dried tomatoes**, finely chopped

1 tablespoon **Dijon mustard**

1 tablespoon light **olive oil**, for cooking

salt and **pepper**

TO SERVE

4 large **burger buns**

rocket

1 quantity **Aïoli** (see page 241)

PREP
25*

COOK
12

SERVES
4

garlicky

Garlic-butter burgers with aïoli

If you don't like too much garlic, serve these mouth-watering burgers with plain mayonnaise or a simple tomato and onion salsa.

1 Mix the butter with the garlic and parsley. When well combined, spoon on to a piece of greaseproof paper and roll up into a thick cylinder shape. Chill for 1 hour.

2 Mix the beef with the sun-dried tomatoes and mustard and season well with salt and pepper. Unwrap the butter and cut it into 4 equal-sized discs. Divide the beef mixture into 4 portions and mould each piece around a disc of butter. Cover and chill for 1 hour.

3 Brush the burgers with a little oil and cook them on an oiled barbecue grill over medium-hot coals for 5–6 minutes on each side, depending on how you like them cooked.

4 To assemble, halve and toast the buns on the barbecue, fill with the garlic burgers and some rocket and serve with the aïoli.

* plus 2 hours chilling

Beef steak burgers with onions

The caramelized onions add sweetness to these juicy, classic burgers.

PREP 10

COOK 35

SERVES 4

classic

1 Gently heat half the oil in a frying pan. Add the onions and cook over a low heat until they are caramelized, about 25 minutes, then set aside.

2 Lightly brush the steaks with the remaining oil and rub the pepper and thyme into the meat. Cook them on an oiled barbecue grill over medium-hot coals for about 4 minutes on each side, depending on how you like them cooked.

3 To assemble, halve and toast the rolls on the barbecue. Top the base of each roll with some watercress, a cooked steak and some of the caramelized onions. Drizzle with the horseradish mayonnaise and stack the parsnip chips on top. Serve the bun lid and extra watercress on the side.

2 tablespoons light **olive oil**

3 **onions**, cut into thin segments

4 small **rib-eye steaks**

1 tablespoon cracked black **pepper**

2 tablespoons chopped **thyme**

TO SERVE

4 **focaccia rolls**

1 bunch of **watercress**

1 quantity **Horseradish Mayonnaise** (see page 238)

1 quantity **Straw Parsnip Chips with Thyme** (see page 194)

625 g (1¼ lb) good-quality coarsely minced **beef**

50 g (2 oz) **quince paste**, finely diced

2 tablespoons chopped **parsley**

1 tablespoon **Dijon mustard**

1 teaspoon **cayenne pepper**

1 tablespoon **Worcestershire sauce**

75 g (3 oz) **Parmesan cheese**, freshly grated

a little light **olive oil**

175 g (6 oz) mature **Cheddar cheese**, cut into thick slices

salt and **pepper**

TO SERVE

4 **crusty rolls**

salad leaves

1 **beef tomato**, sliced

a selection of **pickles**, such as gherkins and pickled onions

1 quantity **Wholegrain Mustard Mayonnaise** (see page 240)

PREP
15*

COOK
12

SERVES
4

tasty

The ultimate cheeseburger

Fresh quince tastes somewhere between an apple and a pear and makes excellent jams and pastes. Quince paste is sweet, with a flowery taste, and can be found on most cheese counters in large supermarkets.

1 Mix together the beef, quince paste, parsley, mustard, cayenne pepper, Worcestershire sauce and Parmesan in a large bowl. Season well with salt and pepper. Divide the mixture into 4 portions and shape each one into a ball, then flatten slightly into a burger. Cover and chill for 30 minutes.

2 Brush the burgers with a little oil and cook them on an oiled barbecue grill over medium-hot coals for 5–6 minutes on each side, depending on how you like them cooked. Towards the end of the cooking time, place the slices of Cheddar cheese on top of the burgers so that they melt slightly in the heat from the barbecue.

3 To assemble, halve and toast the rolls on the barbecue, fill with salad leaves, tomato slices and the burgers and serve with a selection of pickles and wholegrain mustard mayonnaise on the side.

* plus 30 minutes chilling

Smoky beef burgers

Smoked garlic and smoked paprika can be bought in large supermarkets. They add quite a kick to these tasty burgers.

1 Heat 1 tablespoon of oil in a frying pan and fry the onion, garlic, paprika and cumin seeds over a medium heat for 5 minutes until softened. Set aside to cool. Mix together the minced beef, onion mixture and smoked bacon. Season well with salt and pepper. Divide the mixture into 4 portions and shape each one into a ball, then flatten slightly into a burger. Cover and chill for 30 minutes.

2 Brush the burgers with a little oil and cook them on an oiled barbecue grill over medium-hot coals for 5–6 minutes on each side, depending on how you like them cooked. Towards the end of the cooking time, place the slices of mozzarella on top of the burgers so that they melt slightly in the heat from the barbecue.

3 To assemble, halve and toast the rolls on the barbecue, fill with salad leaves, the burgers and some quick BBQ sauce and serve.

1 tablespoon **olive oil**, plus extra for brushing

1 **onion**, finely chopped

2 smoked or fresh **garlic cloves**, crushed

2 teaspoons **smoked paprika**

1 teaspoon **cumin seeds**, crushed

625 g (1¼ lb) good-quality coarsely minced **beef**

200 g (7 oz) **smoked bacon**, finely chopped

125 g (4 oz) **smoked mozzarella**, cut into 4 slices

salt and **pepper**

TO SERVE

4 **crusty rolls**

75 g (3 oz) mixed **salad leaves**

1 quantity **Quick BBQ Sauce** (see page 230)

500 g (1 lb) good-quality coarsely minced **beef**

150 g (5 oz) **pork and herb sausages**, skinned

1 **garlic clove**, crushed

1 tablespoon **Dijon mustard**

2 tablespoons finely chopped **parsley**

a little light **olive oil**, for brushing

salt and **pepper**

CHILLI SAUCE

1 tablespoon light **olive oil**

1 **onion**, finely chopped

1 large **red chilli**, finely chopped

1 teaspoon **paprika**

1 **garlic clove**, crushed

200 g (7 oz) good-quality coarsely minced **beef**

450 ml (14½ fl oz) **passata**

1 tablespoon **Worcestershire sauce**

1 teaspoon **Tabasco sauce**

200 g (7 oz) can **red kidney beans**, drained and rinsed

salt and **pepper**

TO SERVE

4 **ciabatta rolls**

salad leaves

PREP
25*

COOK
40

SERVES
4

hot

Chilli beef burgers

Here juicy burgers are topped with some chilli beef sauce, providing a real meat feast.

1 To make the chilli sauce, heat the oil in a frying pan and cook the onion, chilli, paprika and garlic until soft, about 3–4 minutes. Add the minced beef and cook for 2–3 minutes until browned. Stir in the remaining sauce ingredients, then season with salt and pepper and stir well. Cover and cook over a low heat for 20 minutes.

2 Mix together the beef, sausage-meat, garlic, mustard and parsley in a bowl and season well with salt and pepper. Divide the mixture into 4 portions and shape each one into a ball, then flatten slightly into a burger. Cover and chill for 30 minutes.

3 Brush the burgers with a little oil and cook them on an oiled barbecue grill over medium-hot coals for 5–6 minutes on each side, depending on how you like them cooked.

4 To assemble, halve and toast the rolls on the barbecue, top each base with salad leaves and a burger, spoon over the chilli sauce and serve with the roll lid on the side.

* plus 30 minutes chilling

Aussie burgers

PREP
20*

COOK
20

SERVES
4

tasty

Using crinkle-cut beetroot or other crinkle-cut pickles is an old trick in the making of burgers: it stops the pickles from sliding out of the bun while you are eating it. Simple yet effective.

1 Mix the beef, garlic, onion, mustard, Worcestershire sauce and thyme together in a bowl and season well. Divide the mixture into 4 portions and shape each one into a ball, then flatten slightly into a burger. Cover and chill for 1 hour.

2 Grill the bacon until slightly crisp and keep it warm. Brush the burgers with a little oil and cook them on an oiled barbecue grill over medium-hot coals for 5–6 minutes on each side, depending on how you like them cooked. Keep them warm.

3 Heat some oil in a frying pan and fry the eggs for 3–4 minutes or until the white part of the egg is cooked but the yolk is still soft.

4 To assemble, halve and toast the buns on the barbecue. Layer some salad leaves, the burger, bacon, Cheddar, pineapple, beetroot and egg on the base of each bun and top with the lid. Stick a skewer through the burger to prevent it falling apart and serve topped with the Southern fried onion rings.

625 g (1¼ lb) good-quality coarsely minced **beef**

2 **garlic cloves**, crushed

1 **onion**, finely chopped

1 tablespoon **Dijon mustard**

1 tablespoon **Worcestershire sauce**

1 tablespoon chopped **thyme**

4 **back bacon** rashers

a little light **olive oil**, for brushing and frying

4 **eggs**

salt and **pepper**

TO SERVE

4 **burger buns**

mixed **salad leaves**

4 thin slices of **Cheddar cheese**

4 slices of **pineapple**

8 slices of **pickled beetroot**, crinkle cut

1 quantity **Southern Fried Onion Rings** (see page 196)

750 g (1½ lb) piece **sirloin steak**, trimmed and cut into 16 long thin strips

8 long sprigs of **rosemary**

4 tablespoons **balsamic vinegar**

175 ml (6 fl oz) **red wine**

4 tablespoons **olive oil**

1 tablespoon cracked black **pepper**

salt

HORSERADISH SALSA

250 g (8 oz) **cooked beetroot**, peeled and chopped

½ **red onion**, finely chopped

1–2 tablespoons finely grated **fresh horseradish** or **horseradish relish**, or to taste

salt and **pepper**

PREP
10*

COOK
8

SERVES
4

hot

Beef kebabs

These fragrant rosemary-skewered kebabs look really attractive piled high on a platter with the salsa served on the side in a bowl.

1 Thread 2 pieces of steak on to each sprig of rosemary, in a zig-zag pattern. To make the marinade, mix together the vinegar, wine, olive oil and pepper in a large, shallow non-metallic dish. Add the steak and turn to coat thoroughly. Cover and leave to marinate for 1–2 hours.

2 To make the horseradish salsa, mix the beetroot, onion and horseradish, season and set aside.

3 Remove the kebabs from the marinade, sprinkle with a little salt and cook them on an oiled barbecue grill over medium-hot coals for 3–4 minutes on each side, turning and basting them frequently with the remaining marinade. Serve with the salsa.

* plus 1–2 hours marinating

Shish kebabs

PREP
10*

COOK
8

These classic kebabs always go down well at social gatherings. The aubergines can also be cooked on the barbecue – just drizzle a little olive oil over the top and barbecue until golden.

1 To make the marinade, mix the garlic, grated onions, lemon juice and rind, olive oil, peppercorns and oregano or parsley in a large non-metallic dish. Add the beef cubes and toss to coat thoroughly. Cover and leave to marinate for 2–3 hours.

2 Remove the beef cubes from the marinade and thread on to 4 skewers, alternating with squares of yellow pepper. Cook on an oiled barbecue grill over hot coals for 3–4 minutes on each side, turning and basting frequently with the remaining marinade.

3 Serve with grilled aubergines and couscous, bulgar wheat or rice.

SERVES
4

classic

1–2 **garlic cloves**, crushed

2 **onions**, grated

juice and finely grated rind of 1 **lemon**

75 ml (3 fl oz) **olive oil**

2 teaspoons bottled **green peppercorns**, drained and crushed

2 tablespoons chopped **oregano** or **parsley**

500 g (1 lb) piece of **steak** (e.g. sirloin, rump or fillet), cut into 2.5 cm (1 inch) cubes

1 **yellow pepper**, cored, deseeded and cut into 2.5 cm (1 inch) squares

TO SERVE

grilled aubergines

couscous, **bulgar wheat** or **rice**

Beef satay

100 ml (3½ fl oz) **coconut milk**

2 tablespoons **soy sauce**

1 **red chilli**, finely chopped

2 **garlic cloves**, crushed

grated rind and juice of 1 **lime**

500 g (1 lb) **beef rump steak**, cut lengthways into thin strips

lime wedges, to garnish

TO SERVE

crisp green **salad leaves**

Dipping Sauce (see page 31) or **Satay Sauce** (see page 105)

PREP
15*

COOK
8

SERVES
4

oriental

Just before serving, squeeze the lime wedges over the kebabs. Lime adds a fresh and zesty contrast to the fiery flavour of the chillies.

1 To make the marinade, mix together all the ingredients except for the beef in a large, shallow non-metallic dish. Add the beef strips and turn to coat thoroughly. Cover and leave to marinate in the refrigerator for at least 4 hours.

2 Remove the beef from the marinade and thread in a zig-zag pattern on to 8 skewers. Cook on an oiled barbecue grill over hot coals for 3–4 minutes on each side, turning and basting frequently with the remaining marinade.

3 Serve the beef strips on crisp green salad leaves with some dipping sauce or satay sauce and garnished with lime wedges.

* plus 4 hours marinating

Grilled lemon grass beef

This recipe also works wonderfully well with chicken or pork. Use the same quantity of meat and cut it into even cubes.

1 To make the marinade, pound together the lemon grass, shallots, chillies, garlic, salt, pepper and oil using a mortar and pestle, or process in a small food processor. Tip into a large non-metallic dish, add the beef and toss to coat thoroughly. Cover and leave to marinate for at least 3 hours.

2 Meanwhile, to make the dipping sauce, mix all the ingredients together in a bowl and stir until the sugar has dissolved.

3 Remove the beef from the marinade and thread on to 8 skewers. Cook on an oiled barbecue grill over hot coals for about 3 minutes on each side, turning occasionally. Serve with the salad, dipping sauce and pieces of French bread.

4 **lemon grass stalks**, finely chopped

4 large **shallots**, finely chopped

2 small **red chillies**, finely chopped

3 large **garlic cloves**, finely chopped

1 teaspoon **salt**

1 teaspoon **pepper**

1 tablespoon **groundnut oil**

750 g (1½ lb) **lean rump steak**, cut into 1 cm (½ inch) cubes

DIPPING SAUCE

3 tablespoons **white wine** or **Chinese rice wine vinegar**

3 tablespoons dark **soy sauce**

1½ teaspoons **caster sugar**

2 small **red chillies**, finely sliced

TO SERVE

herb salad

French bread

Satay lembu

300 ml (½ pint) **coconut milk**

2 **garlic cloves**, crushed

pinch of **ground cardamom**

pinch of **ground cinnamon**

pinch of **ground cumin**

pinch of **curry powder**

2 teaspoons chopped fresh **root ginger**

freshly ground black **pepper**

625 g (1¼ lb) **rump steak**, cut into 5 cm (2 inch) cubes

Satay Sauce (see page 105), to serve

TO GARNISH

lime wedges

sprigs of **mint**

PREP
10*

COOK
8

SERVES
4

spicy

These barbecued skewers are full of Malayan aromatic flavours. These ingredients will also serve 8 as a starter: cut the meat into 2.5 cm (1 inch) pieces and cook for just 2–3 minutes on each side.

1 To make the marinade, mix together the coconut milk, garlic, cardamom, cinnamon, cumin, curry powder, ginger and black pepper in a large non-metallic dish. Add the steak cubes and turn to coat thoroughly. Cover and leave to marinate in the refrigerator for 4–6 hours.

2 Remove the steak cubes from the marinade and thread on to 8 skewers; drain well. Cook on an oiled barbecue grill over hot coals for 3–4 minutes on each side. Serve garnished with lime wedges and mint sprigs, accompanied by the satay sauce.

* plus 4–6 hours
marinating

Peppered steaks

PREP
30

COOK
60

SERVES
4

tasty

This dish is simplicity itself, but when served with a classic tomato sauce it turns into something really special. Guaranteed to please all ages!

1 To make the tomato and garlic sauce, cut the tomatoes in half lengthways and scoop out the seeds with a spoon. Lightly grease a baking sheet with a little of the olive oil and lay the tomatoes on top, cut side up, with the garlic cloves. Drizzle with the remaining olive oil.

2 Sprinkle the salt and sugar evenly over the tomatoes and place in a preheated oven, 180°C (350°F), Gas Mark 4, for 45–50 minutes. Remove the garlic cloves after 15 minutes or when the flesh is very soft. When cool enough to handle, pop the garlic flesh out of its skins and set aside.

3 Place the tomatoes, with any juices that have accumulated, and the garlic flesh in a food processor or blender and process until smooth. Strain through a sieve into a clean pan, season to taste and reheat when ready to serve.

4 To prepare the steaks, mix together the crushed peppercorns and olive oil on a plate. Dip each steak into the peppercorn oil and coat evenly on both sides. Cook the steaks on an oiled barbecue grill over medium-hot coals for 2–3 minutes on each side for rare, 3–4 minutes for medium rare, 4–5 minutes for medium or 5–6 minutes for well done.

5 Serve with the tomato and garlic sauce.

2 tablespoons **mixed peppercorns**, well crushed

3 tablespoons **olive oil**

4 **fillet steaks**, about 175 g (6 oz) each

TOMATO AND
GARLIC SAUCE

1 kg (2 lb) ripe **tomatoes**, preferably plum

3 tablespoons **extra virgin olive oil**

8 **garlic cloves**, unpeeled

1 teaspoon **sea salt**

2 teaspoons **caster sugar**

4 **fillet steaks**, about 250 g (8 oz) each

2 **red onions**, thinly sliced into rings

3 tablespoons **balsamic vinegar**

50 ml (2 fl oz) **red wine**

2 tablespoons **olive oil**

1–2 **garlic cloves**, crushed

salt and **pepper**

tomato and onion salad, to serve

PREP
10*

COOK
30

SERVES
4

intense

Balsamic steaks

Rich, dark, Italian balsamic vinegar is used in this marinade for barbecued fillet steaks.

1 Place the steaks in a large, shallow non-metallic dish and sprinkle the red onion rings over the top. To make the marinade, mix together the balsamic vinegar, red wine, 2 tablespoons of olive oil, garlic and season, then pour over the steaks. Turn to coat thoroughly. Cover and marinate for 1–1½ hours, turning once.

2 Remove the steaks from the marinade, cover and set aside. Tip the marinade, including the onions, into a saucepan. Bring to the boil, then reduce the heat and simmer until it is reduced by about half. Place the pan on the side of the barbecue to keep warm while you cook the steaks.

3 Cook the steaks on an oiled barbecue grill over hot coals for 2–3 minutes on each side for very rare, 3–4 minutes for rare, 4–5 minutes for medium rare. Spoon over the sauce and serve immediately with a tomato and onion salad.

* plus 1–1½ hours marinating

The great steak sandwich

This sandwich with its sweet onion purée, succulent steak, creamy fontina cheese, tomato and rocket, is a meal in itself. The onion purée can be made the day before, if you like.

1   Heat 4 tablespoons of the olive oil in a frying pan, add the mustard seeds, cover and let them pop for 30 seconds over moderate heat – but do not let them burn. Add the onions and garlic and cook over a very low heat for 30 minutes until they are very soft but not coloured.

2   Purée the softened onion mixture in a food processor or blender, then spoon into a bowl. Stir in the parsley and vinegar, with salt and pepper to taste. Cover and set aside.

3   Brush the steaks with a little of the remaining oil. Season with crushed black peppercorns. Cook them on an oiled barbecue grill over hot coals for 2–3 minutes on each side for very rare, up to 5–6 minutes for medium or 10–12 minutes if you like meat well done.

4   Toast the bread slices on both sides on the barbecue and spread with the onion purée. Slice the steaks thinly and divide between 4 of the bread slices. Top with the fontina, tomato slices and rocket. Season with salt and pepper, top with the remaining bread slices and serve at once.

PREP
15

COOK
40–55

SERVES
4

juicy

6 tablespoons **olive oil**

2 teaspoons **mustard seeds**

2 large **red onions**, thinly sliced

2 **garlic cloves**, crushed

15 g (½ oz) **flat leaf parsley**, chopped

1 tablespoon **balsamic vinegar**

2 **rump** or **sirloin steaks**, about 250 g (8 oz) each

crushed **black peppercorns**

8 slices of **olive bread** or **crusty bread**

75 g (3 oz) **fontina cheese**, thinly sliced

2 ripe **beefsteak tomatoes**, sliced

125 g (4 oz) **rocket**

sea salt and **pepper**

375 g (12 oz) **calves' liver**, sliced and skinned

6–8 slices of **prosciutto**

2 tablespoons **thyme leaves**

16 **bay leaves**

2 tablespoons **olive oil**

salt and **pepper**

ONION RELISH

50 g (2 oz) **butter**

4 large **red onions**, sliced

2 tablespoons **thyme leaves**

1 tablespoon **red wine vinegar**

1 tablespoon **caster sugar**

PREP
30

COOK
45

SERVES
4

tender

Calves' liver and prosciutto kebabs

Calves' liver should always be cooked quickly so that it is tender and juicy in the middle and browned on the outside.

1 Melt the butter in a large frying pan. Stir in the onions and thyme and cover the pan, then cook the onions gently for 40 minutes, until softened but not coloured, stirring once.

2 Meanwhile, cut the calves' liver and prosciutto into 7 x 2.5 cm (3 x 1 inch) slices. Place a strip of prosciutto on each piece of liver, then sprinkle with a little thyme and season with salt and pepper.

3 Roll up from the short end and thread on to a skewer. Repeat with the remaining calves' liver and prosciutto until all the skewers have been filled, adding bay leaves at regular intervals. Brush the kebabs with the olive oil.

4 Cook the kebabs on an oiled barbecue grill over hot coals for about 5–6 minutes, turning frequently.

5 Meanwhile, remove the lid from the frying pan and stir in the vinegar and sugar, then increase the heat and boil rapidly to reduce the juices. Spoon into a bowl and serve with the kebabs.

Indian-spiced lamb burgers

PREP
25*

COOK
17

SERVES
4

spicy

A hot alternative to the classic burger. Children love these spicy burgers, especially when served with naan bread, poppadums and mango chutney.

1 Heat the oil in a frying pan and fry the onion, garlic, chilli, mustard seeds and spices for 5 minutes or until the onion has softened and the mustard seeds start to pop. Set aside to cool.

2 Mix together the lamb, breadcrumbs, egg and onion mixture in a large bowl and season with salt and pepper. Divide the mixture into 8 portions and shape each one into a ball, then flatten slightly into a burger. Cover and chill for 30 minutes.

3 Brush the burgers with a little oil and cook them on an oiled barbecue grill over hot coals for 5–6 minutes on each side, depending on how you like them cooked.

4 To assemble, toast the naan breads on the barbecue until lightly browned. Top each naan with some coriander, a sprinkling of red chilli powder, if using, a burger and some cucumber and tomato cubes. Serve the burgers with mango chutney and the mini poppadums.

2 tablespoons light **olive oil**, plus extra for brushing

1 **onion**

2 **garlic cloves**, crushed

1 **red chilli**, deseeded and finely chopped

1 teaspoon **black mustard seeds**

1 tablespoon **garam masala**

1 teaspoon **turmeric**

625 g (1¼ lb) good-quality coarsely minced **lamb**

50 g (2 oz) **breadcrumbs**

1 **egg**

salt and **pepper**

TO SERVE

8 **mini naan breads**

1 small bunch of **coriander**, chopped

red chilli powder (optional)

½ **cucumber**, cubed

2 **tomatoes**, cubed

mango chutney

mini poppadums

* plus 30 minutes chilling

625 g (1¼ lb) good-quality coarsely minced **lamb**

2 **garlic cloves**, crushed

grated rind of 1 **lemon**

150 g (5 oz) **feta cheese**, diced

50 g (2 oz) **black olives**, chopped

50 g (2 oz) **pine nuts**, dry-roasted and chopped

3 tablespoons chopped **oregano**

a little light **olive oil**, for brushing

TO SERVE

4 **floured rolls**

3 **tomatoes**, cut into wedges

½ **cucumber**, cut into ribbons with a vegetable peeler

50 g (2 oz) **Kalamata olives**

1 tablespoon chopped **flat leaf parsley**

pine nuts

Greek yogurt

lemon wedges

PREP
20*

COOK
12

SERVES
4

herby

Greek-style lamb burgers

A taste of the Mediterranean in a burger. The fresh combination of lemon, garlic and olives mixes with the lamb to create perfect food for outdoor eating.

1 Mix together all the ingredients for the burgers except the oil in a bowl and season well. Divide the mixture into 4 portions and shape each one into a ball, then flatten slightly into a burger. Cover and chill for 30 minutes.

2 Brush the burgers with a little oil and cook them on an oiled barbecue grill over hot coals for 5–6 minutes on each side, depending on how you like them cooked.

3 To assemble, halve and toast the rolls on the barbecue, fill with some tomato, cucumber, olives and parsley, the burgers and pine nuts and serve with Greek yogurt and lemon wedges.

* plus 30 minutes chilling

Lamb fillet burgers

If you don't want your crisply toasted buns to go soggy, serve the mint dressing separately as a dipping sauce.

1 To make the marinade, mix together all the ingredients except for the lamb and aubergine in a large, shallow non-metallic dish and season well with salt and pepper. Add the lamb steaks and aubergine slices and turn to coat thoroughly. Cover and leave to marinate for 1 hour.

2 Remove the steaks and aubergine slices from the marinade and cook on an oiled barbecue grill over medium-hot coals for about 4 minutes on each side, depending on how you like them cooked, turning and basting them frequently with the remaining marinade.

3 To make the mint dressing, mix together all the ingredients and season to taste with salt and pepper.

4 To assemble, halve and lightly toast the buns on the barbecue, then top each base with some salad leaves, 2 aubergine slices, more salad leaves, then a lamb steak. Drizzle with the mint dressing and top with the bun lid.

PREP
20*

COOK
8

SERVES
4

minty

3 teaspoons **ground cumin**

2 teaspoons **ground coriander**

2 **garlic cloves**, crushed

2 tablespoons finely chopped **mint**

grated rind of 1 **lemon**

75 ml (3 fl oz) **olive oil**

4 **lamb leg steaks**, about 150 g (5 oz) each

1 small **aubergine**, cut into 8 slices

salt and **pepper**

MINT DRESSING

125 ml (4 fl oz) **Greek yogurt**

1 **garlic clove**, crushed

2 tablespoons chopped **mint**

juice of 1 **lemon**

salt and **pepper**

TO SERVE

4 **burger buns**

salad leaves

625 g (1¼ lb) good-quality coarsely minced **lamb**

75 g (3 oz) **dried apricots**, finely chopped

3 tablespoons finely chopped **coriander**

2 tablespoons finely chopped **flat leaf parsley**

2 **garlic cloves**, crushed

2 teaspoons **ground cumin**

½ teaspoon **cayenne pepper**

½ teaspoon **turmeric**

a little light **olive oil**, for brushing

salt and **pepper**

SLOW-ROASTED TOMATOES

6 **Roma tomatoes** or **plum tomatoes**, halved

large pinch of **paprika**

2 **garlic cloves**, chopped

1 tablespoon **olive oil**

salt and **pepper**

TO SERVE

4 **soft rolls**

salad leaves

PREP
12*

COOK
75

SERVES
4

spicy

Chermoula lamb burgers

Chermoula is traditionally used in Moroccan cooking as a marinade and sauce for fish, but its strong flavours also go well with meat, as in this lamb burger recipe.

1 To prepare the roasted tomatoes, place the tomatoes cut side up on a lightly greased nonstick baking sheet. Sprinkle over the paprika and chopped garlic and season well with salt and pepper. Drizzle with olive oil and roast in a preheated oven, 150°C (300°F), Gas Mark 2, for 1 hour. Remove and set aside until needed.

2 Mix all the burger ingredients except the oil in a large bowl and season well with salt and pepper. Divide the mixture into 4 portions and shape each one into a ball, then flatten slightly into a burger. Cover and chill for 30 minutes.

3 Brush the burgers with a little oil and cook them on an oiled barbecue grill over medium-hot coals for 5–6 minutes on each side, depending on how you like them cooked.

4 To assemble, halve and toast the rolls on the barbecue, then fill with salad leaves, a burger and 3 roasted tomatoes.

* plus 30 minutes
chilling

Kofta kebabs

PREP
20

COOK
12

SERVES
8

fragrant

This speciality from the Middle East consists of spiced minced lamb or beef pressed around skewers, grilled and served with a minty yogurt dip. Metal skewers are most authentic.

1 To make the dip, mix the yogurt, chopped tomatoes and mint in a bowl and season with the cayenne and salt. Cover the bowl and place in the refrigerator until required.

2 Place the pine nuts in a frying pan over a medium heat and dry-fry, stirring continuously, for a minute or two until they are golden brown.

3 Place the minced lamb or beef in a food processor or blender and work it into a smooth paste. Alternatively, pass it through the finest blade of a mincer. Scrape the mixture into a bowl and stir in the onion, pine nuts, oregano and spices. Season with salt and pepper.

4 Mould the mixture around 8 skewers, forming it into flat sausage shapes. Cook the skewers on an oiled barbecue grill over hot coals for about 10–12 minutes, turning frequently, until the meat is browned all over and cooked through.

5 Remove the kebabs from the skewers and serve with the pitta chips, Cos lettuce and yogurt dip.

125 g (4 oz) **pine nuts**

1 kg (2 lb) good-quality coarsely minced **lamb** or **beef**

2 **onions**, grated

2 tablespoons chopped **oregano**

1 teaspoon **ground cumin**

1 teaspoon **ground coriander**

salt and **pepper**

YOGURT DIP

600 ml (1 pint) **Greek yogurt**

6 **tomatoes**, skinned (see page 13), deseeded and chopped

2 tablespoons chopped **mint**

¼ teaspoon **cayenne pepper**

salt

TO SERVE
Pitta Chips (see page 201)

Cos lettuce

2 **green chillies**, deseeded and finely chopped

1 teaspoon grated fresh **root ginger**

2 **garlic cloves**, crushed

3 tablespoons chopped **coriander**

2 tablespoons chopped **mint leaves**

1 teaspoon **cumin seeds**

1 tablespoon **vegetable oil**

½ teaspoon **ground cloves**

½ teaspoon **ground cardamom seeds**

500 g (1 lb) good-quality coarsely minced **lamb**

a little **oil**, for brushing

sea salt

PREP
10*

COOK
8

SERVES
12

hot

Sheekh kebabs

These kebabs are popular in India. Barbecued over charcoal braziers, they are eaten with onions, mint and hot bread. The meat mixture can be formed into balls and threaded on to skewers with onion or pepper.

1 Put the chillies, ginger, garlic, coriander, mint, cumin, oil, ground cloves and cardamom into a food processor or blender and process until fairly smooth. Transfer to a mixing bowl, add the lamb and salt and mix well, using your hands. Divide the mixture into 12 portions, cover and chill for 30 minutes, if time allows.

2 Lightly brush a little oil on to 12 flat metal skewers and shape a portion of the kebab mixture around each skewer, forming a sausage shape.

3 Cook the kebabs on an oiled barbecue grill over hot coals for 3–4 minutes on each side, or until cooked through and browned.

* plus 30 minutes chilling (optional)

Kidney and bacon kebabs

PREP
15

COOK
8

SERVES
4

herby

The pancetta will help to baste the kidneys and prevent them from drying out, while the sage gives the meat a delicious flavour.

1 Split the kidneys in half and carefully remove the core and fat. Score the rounded side of each half kidney in a criss-cross pattern. Wrap a slice of pancetta around each piece.

2 Cut the onion into wedges, taking care to keep the root end intact so that the leaves of the onion are held together

3 Thread the pieces of kidney and bacon on to 4 skewers, alternating them with red onion wedges and sage leaves.

4 Season the kebabs with salt and pepper, brush with melted butter and cook on an oiled barbecue grill over hot coals for 3–4 minutes on each side, basting frequently with the remaining butter.

6 **lambs' kidneys**

6 slices of **pancetta** or rindless **streaky bacon**, halved

1 **red onion**

1 bunch of **sage**, leaves stripped from the stalks

50 g (2 oz) **butter**, melted

salt and **pepper**

8 **lamb noisettes**

2 tablespoons **olive oil**

pepper

MINT PESTO

25 g (1 oz) **mint**

15 g (½ oz) **flat leaf parsley**

25 g (1 oz) **pistachio nuts**, shelled

2 **garlic cloves**

125 ml (4 fl oz) **olive oil**

25 g (1 oz) **Parmesan cheese**, grated

salt and **pepper**

grilled courgettes, to serve

PREP
30

COOK
10

SERVES
4

tender

Lamb noisettes with mint pesto

Noisettes are a very tender, boneless cut of lamb, not less than 1 cm (½ inch) thick, from the loin or best end of neck. They are usually cut by the butcher. Mint pesto goes with them perfectly.

1 To make the mint pesto, place the mint, parsley, pistachios and garlic in a food processor or blender and process until finely chopped. With the motor running, gradually add the olive oil in a thin, steady stream until amalgamated. Pour the pesto into a bowl, stir in the Parmesan and season with salt and pepper to taste.

2 Brush the noisettes with olive oil, sprinkle with pepper and cook on an oiled barbecue grill over hot coals for 4–5 minutes on each side.

3 Place the noisettes on individual plates, spoon over the pesto and serve. Grilled courgettes and their flowers are a suitable accompaniment.

Lamb loin chops with chutney

Loin chops should be cooked quickly on the barbecue, until golden and crispy on the outside, but still slightly pink on the inside.

PREP
5*

COOK
10

SERVES
4

spicy

1 To make the marinade, mix together the garlic, ginger, oil and spices in a large, shallow non-metallic dish. Add the lamb and rub thoroughly with the marinade. Cover and leave to marinate for 2–3 hours, turning from time to time.

2 To make the coriander chutney, place all the ingredients in a food processor or blender and blend until smooth. Stop the machine every so often and push down any bits with a spatula and blend again. Turn into a small bowl to serve.

3 Place each lamb chop on a skewer. Pull the onion wedges apart and thread a few pieces on to the skewer with the chop.

4 Season the skewers with a little salt, place on an oiled barbecue grill over hot coals and cook for 4–5 minutes on each side. Serve with the chutney and a green salad.

2 **garlic cloves**, crushed

2.5 cm (1 inch) piece of fresh **root ginger**, crushed in a garlic press

2 tablespoons **sunflower oil** or **vegetable oil**

2 teaspoons **ground coriander**

1 teaspoon **ground cumin**

½ teaspoon **ground cloves**

¼ teaspoon **ground cinnamon**

¼ teaspoon **pepper**

4 **lamb loin chops**

1 **red onion**, cut into 8 wedges

½ teaspoon **salt**

green salad, to serve

CORIANDER CHUTNEY

8 tablespoons chopped **coriander**

1 small **green chilli**, deseeded and finely chopped

1 teaspoon **garam masala**

1 teaspoon **sugar**

1 teaspoon **salt**

2 tablespoons **lime** or **lemon juice**

juice and finely grated rind of ½ **lemon**

1 **garlic clove**, crushed

4 sprigs of **rosemary**, finely chopped

4 **anchovy fillets** in oil, drained and finely chopped

2 tablespoons **extra virgin olive oil**

2 tablespoons **lemon cordial**

12 **lamb cutlets**, trimmed of all fat

salt and **pepper**

PREP
5*

COOK
10

SERVES
4

juicy

Lamb cutlets with lemon and rosemary

It is important to use lean lamb for barbecuing because excess fat will drip on to the coals and cause flare-ups and burnt food.

1 To make the marinade, mix together the lemon rind and juice, garlic, rosemary, anchovies, olive oil and lemon cordial in a large, shallow non-metallic dish and season with salt and pepper. Add the lamb cutlets and turn to coat thoroughly. Cover and leave to marinate for 15 minutes.

2 Remove the lamb from the marinade and cook on an oiled barbecue grill over hot coals for 3–5 minutes on each side, until charred and cooked through. Leave to rest for a few minutes and serve.

* plus 15 minutes marinating

Jerk pork burgers with mango salsa

Marinated roasted peppers are available in the deli sections at most supermarkets or they can be bought, preserved, in jars.

PREP
25*

COOK
12

SERVES
4

spicy

1 Mix together all the ingredients for the burgers except the oil in a large bowl. Season well with salt and pepper. Divide the mixture into 4 portions and shape each one into a ball, then flatten slightly into a burger. Cover and chill for 30 minutes.

2 To make the salsa, mix together all the ingredients and set aside for at least 30 minutes to allow the flavours to develop.

3 Brush the burgers with a little oil and cook them on an oiled barbecue grill over medium-hot coals for 5–6 minutes on each side, until they are cooked through.

4 To assemble, halve and toast the buns on the barbecue. Top each base with salad leaves, roasted pepper and a burger. Spoon over the salsa and top with the lid.

625 g (1¼ lb) good-quality coarsely minced **pork**

2 tablespoons **jerk seasoning**

grated rind of 1 **lime**

2.5 cm (1 inch) piece of fresh **root ginger**, grated

2 **garlic cloves**, crushed

4 **spring onions**, finely chopped

1 tablespoon **thyme**

a little light **olive oil**, for brushing

salt and **pepper**

MANGO SALSA

1 **mango**, peeled, cored and finely diced

½ **red onion**, peeled, finely diced

1 **red chilli**, deseeded and finely diced

2 tablespoons chopped **mint**

1 tablespoon chopped **coriander**

2 tablespoons **olive oil**

grated rind and juice of 1 **lime**

TO SERVE

4 **burger buns**

salad leaves

4 large pieces of **marinated roasted red pepper**

* plus 30 minutes chilling and standing

25 g (1 oz) **butter**

1 **leek**, finely chopped

1 **cooking apple**, peeled and grated

2 **garlic cloves**, crushed

1 teaspoon **mace**

1 tablespoon chopped **rosemary**

625 g (1¼ lb) minced **pork**

a little **oil**, for brushing

salt and **pepper**

APPLE BALSAMIC RELISH

2 **apples**, chopped

250 g (8 oz) **baby plum tomatoes**

1 **red onion**, chopped

2 **garlic cloves**, chopped

1 tablespoon **green peppercorns**

3 sprigs of **thyme**

1 teaspoon **rock salt**

50 g (2 oz) **sugar**

50 ml (2 fl oz) **balsamic vinegar**

200 ml (7 fl oz) **apple cider**

TO SERVE

4 **crusty rolls**

salad leaves

1 **red onion**, thinly sliced into rings

PREP
20*

COOK
40

SERVES
4

moist

Pork, leek and apple burgers

The leek and apple add an unusual flavour and help to keep these burgers moist and juicy. There's more apple, and cider too, in the accompanying relish, which can be made well ahead of time.

1 Melt the butter in a frying pan and fry the leek, apple, garlic and mace over a medium heat for 4–5 minutes until tender. Add the rosemary, remove from the heat and leave to cool.

2 Mix together the minced pork and the leek mixture and season well with salt and pepper. Divide the mixture into 4 portions and shape each one into a ball, then flatten slightly into a burger. Cover and chill for 30 minutes.

3 Meanwhile, to make the apple balsamic relish, place all the ingredients in a large heavy-based pan and gently bring them to the boil. Simmer over a medium heat for 25 minutes, stirring occasionally until the mixture is thick.

4 Brush the burgers with a little oil and cook them on an oiled barbecue grill over medium-hot coals for 5–6 minutes on each side, until cooked through.

5 To assemble, halve and toast the rolls on the barbecue and fill with lots of salad leaves, onion rings and the burger. Top with spoonfuls of apple balsamic relish and serve immediately.

* plus 30 minutes chilling

Hanoi grilled pork

This dish can be found for sale on street corners all over Asia. It makes for an equally delicious barbecue dinner served in a bowl with noodles.

1 Gently melt the light muscovado sugar with two-thirds of the fish sauce in a heavy-based saucepan, stirring all the time. Allow to cool a little, then transfer to a bowl and combine with the garlic, shallot, palm or caster sugar, the remaining fish sauce and salt. Add the minced pork, mix thoroughly, then cover and leave to stand for 3 hours.

2 Shape the minced pork into 20–24 flat little patties, about 2.5 cm (1 inch) in diameter, then cook on an oiled barbecue grill over medium-hot coals for 3–4 minutes on each side, making sure they are cooked right through.

3 To serve, divide the noodles between 4 warmed bowls, then add the pork, the torn lettuce leaves, bean sprouts and herbs. Spoon the dipping sauce over everything.

oriental

1 tablespoon **light muscovado sugar**

2 tablespoons **Thai fish sauce**

1 large **garlic clove**, finely chopped

1 large **shallot**, finely chopped

2 teaspoons **palm sugar** or **golden caster sugar**

1 teaspoon **salt**

500 g (1 lb) boneless **pork loin**, minced

TO SERVE

250 g (8 oz) **rice noodles**, cooked

lettuce leaves, torn

125 g (4 oz) **bean sprouts**

handful of **coriander, basil leaves, mint leaves** and **chives**

Dipping Sauce (see page 31)

sausage casings

500 g (1 lb) lean **shoulder pork**

175 g (6 oz) **back fat** without rind

1½ tablespoons coarse **sea salt**

4 tablespoons **thyme leaves**

½ teaspoon **ground bay leaves**

pepper

MUSTARD AÏOLI

4–6 **garlic cloves**, crushed

2 **egg yolks**

2 tablespoons **lemon juice**, plus extra to taste

300 ml (½ pint) **extra virgin olive oil**

2 tablespoons **coarse-grain mustard**

salt and **pepper**

PREP
60*

COOK
15

SERVES
4

rustic

Homemade sausages with mustard aïoli

Use the sausage-meat mixture to make small patties rather than sausages with skins, if you prefer. Cook these as you would burgers.

1 Soak the casings in cold water for 20 minutes and untangle any knots, then rinse by pulling one end of the casing over the end of the tap and running cold water through it.

2 Trim any skin or gristle from the shoulder and back fat and cut into pieces. Pass the meat through the medium blade of a mincer or finely chop it by hand. Place the meat in a large bowl and add the back fat, sea salt, thyme, bay and pepper. Mix well.

3 Spoon the meat into a large piping bag with a large plastic nozzle and squeeze to remove any excess air. Wriggle the open end of a casing on to and up the nozzle and, holding the skin on to the nozzle, squeeze the filling into the casing to create a long sausage. Twist or knot the long sausage at intervals to make 8 large or 12 small sausages. Separate the sausages with a knife or scissors.

4 Cook the sausages on an oiled barbecue grill over medium coals for 10–15 minutes until cooked through, turning frequently.

5 Meanwhile, make the mustard aïoli. Briefly whizz the garlic, egg yolks and lemon juice in a food processor. With the motor running, add the olive oil in a thin, steady stream until it forms a thick cream. Scrape into a bowl, season and stir in the mustard.

* plus 20 minutes soaking

Pork and juniper kebabs

PREP
15*

COOK
20

SERVES
4

fruity

Juniper adds an unusual fragrant flavour to these kebabs. If you can't buy red grapefruit try pink grapefruit instead – it's equally delicious.

1 To make the marinade, squeeze the juice from one of the grapefruit into a large, shallow non-metallic dish. Add the lime juice, honey, garlic, juniper berries, oil and pepper and mix well. Add the pork cubes and turn to coat thoroughly. Cover and leave to marinate for 1–2 hours.

2 Meanwhile, peel and segment the remaining grapefruit, working over a bowl so that no juice is wasted. Chop the grapefruit segments and place them in the bowl, stir in the chives and onion, season and set the salsa aside.

3 Remove the pork from the marinade and thread on to 4 skewers, placing a bay leaf between each piece of meat.

4 Cook the kebabs on an oiled barbecue grill over medium-hot coals for 15–20 minutes, turning and basting frequently with the remaining marinade. Serve with the grapefruit salsa.

3 **ruby red grapefruit**

2 tablespoons **lime juice**

3 tablespoons **honey**

2 **garlic cloves**, crushed

6 **juniper berries**, finely crushed

100 ml (3½ fl oz) **walnut oil** or **olive oil**

500 g (1 lb) **pork fillet**, trimmed and cut into 4 cm (1½ inch) cubes

2 tablespoons chopped **chives**

2 tablespoons very finely chopped **red onion**

16 **bay leaves**

pepper

* plus 1–2 hours marinating

2 teaspoons **mustard seeds**

6 tablespoons **tamarind paste** or 4 tablespoons **lime juice** or **lemon juice**

4 **garlic cloves**, crushed

2 tablespoons light **soy sauce**

12 tablespoons **honey**

2 teaspoons **ground cumin**

2 teaspoons **ground coriander**

1 teaspoon **chilli powder**

2 kg (4 lb) meaty **pork spare ribs**

MINT RELISH

125 g (4 oz) **mint**, chopped

1 small **red onion**, very finely chopped

2 small **green chillies**, deseeded and chopped

4 tablespoons **lemon juice**

2 teaspoons **caster sugar**

salt and **pepper**

Tamarind spare ribs with mint relish

This marinade can also be used on pork or lamb chops or cutlets. The mint relish adds a sweet tanginess that contrasts well with the marinade.

1 Heat a frying pan over a low heat and dry-fry the mustard seeds until they start to pop. Remove the pan from the heat and leave the seeds to cool, then crush lightly.

2 To make the marinade, mix the crushed mustard seeds and all the remaining ingredients except for the pork in a large, shallow non-metallic dish. Add the spare ribs and turn to coat thoroughly. Cover and leave to marinate for 1–2 hours.

3 To make the mint relish, place the mint, onion, chilli, lemon juice and sugar in a food processor or blender. Work until smooth, pushing it down with a spatula occasionally. Turn out the relish into a bowl and season to taste with salt and pepper.

4 Remove the spare ribs from the marinade and cook on an oiled barbecue grill over medium-hot coals for 15–20 minutes, turning and basting frequently with the remaining marinade. Serve with the mint relish.

* plus 1–2 hours marinating

Spare ribs with ginger

PREP
10

COOK
20

SERVES
4–6

sticky

Make more of these sweet, sticky ribs than you think you could ever need – they seem to disappear rather fast.

1   Arrange the spare ribs on an oiled barbecue grill set 10 cm (4 inches) above hot coals and cook them for 5 minutes, turning occasionally.

2   Put all the remaining ingredients in a saucepan over a low heat, gradually bring to the boil and cook for 1 minute.

3   Remove the ribs from the barbecue and place in a shallow dish. Spoon the sauce over the ribs, and turn to cover them all well. Return the ribs to the barbecue and cook for 10–15 minutes, basting frequently.

1 kg (2 lb) **pork spare ribs**

2 **spring onions**, chopped

1 **garlic clove**, finely sliced

2.5 cm (1 inch) piece of fresh **root ginger**, shredded

1 tablespoon **soy sauce**

4 tablespoons clear **honey**

3 tablespoons **lemon juice**

2 tablespoons **mango chutney**

½ teaspoon **ground ginger**

1 tablespoon **oil**

2 tablespoons **dry sherry**

3 **garlic cloves**

2 tablespoons **palm sugar** or **light muscovado sugar**

15 **black peppercorns**

1 **lemon grass stalk**, roughly chopped

2 tablespoons **Thai fish sauce**

1 tablespoon **Chinese rice wine**

1 teaspoon **sesame oil**

2 tablespoons **groundnut oil**

4 **loin pork chops**, about 250 g (8 oz) each

sprigs of **coriander**, to garnish

PREP
10*

COOK
16

SERVES
4

intense

Spicy Asian pork chops

Palm sugar is a hard brown sugar often sold in round tablets. It is used in many Asian dishes and can be bought in Asian stores or international supermarkets.

1 To make the marinade, put the garlic, sugar, peppercorns, lemon grass, fish sauce, rice wine, sesame oil and groundnut oil into a small food processor and work to a paste. If you prefer, you can pound the first 4 ingredients to a paste in a mortar and add the next 4 ingredients to the paste, little by little, as you pound it. Mix it all thoroughly.

2 Place the pork chops in a large, shallow non-metallic dish and cover them completely with the marinade. Cover and leave to marinate in the refrigerator overnight.

3 Remove the chops from the marinade and cook on an oiled barbecue grill over medium coals for about 8 minutes on each side, until lightly browned and cooked through. Serve the chops garnished with coriander sprigs.

* plus overnight marinating

Prosciutto with balsamic figs

PREP
10

COOK
5

SERVES
4

easy

This is quick to cook on the barbecue. The balsamic vinegar caramelizes on the figs, giving a sweet and sour flavour. If you can't get fresh figs, use peaches. Halve and stone the peaches and cook cut side down.

1 Take the figs one at a time and stand them upright. Using a sharp knife, make 2 cuts through each fig, not quite quartering them but keeping them intact. Ease the figs open and brush with the balsamic vinegar and olive oil.

2 Place the figs, cut side down, on an oiled barbecue grill and cook over medium-hot coals for 3–4 minutes until hot and slightly charred.

3 While the figs are cooking, place half of the slices of prosciutto on the barbecue and cook until frazzled and starting to crisp. Remove and keep warm while cooking the remaining prosciutto.

4 To serve, arrange 3 pieces of prosciutto and 2 figs each on 4 warmed plates. Cover with Parmesan shavings, drizzle with a little more olive oil and sprinkle with plenty of crushed black pepper.

8 ripe **figs**

2 tablespoons **balsamic vinegar**

2 tablespoons **extra virgin olive oil**, plus extra to serve

12 slices of **prosciutto**

TO SERVE

Parmesan cheese shavings

crushed black **pepper**

6 slices of **prosciutto**, cut in half lengthways

2 ripe **pears**, peeled, cored and cut into 6 wedges each

TO SERVE

salad leaves

shavings of **pecorino** or **Parmesan**

cracked black **pepper**

extra virgin olive oil

Prosciutto and pear sticks

So simple, yet delicious and impressive – everything can be prepared and made in a matter of minutes. Serve the pear sticks on a bed of Italian salad leaves.

1 Wrap a piece of prosciutto around each pear wedge and thread 3 wedges on to each of 4 skewers.

2 Place the skewers on an oiled barbecue grill and cook over medium-hot coals for 2–3 minutes on each side. Serve at once on a bed of salad leaves with the cheese shavings, some cracked black pepper and a drizzle of olive oil.

Venison with red juniper pears

Pears in red wine, usually seen as a dessert, are also wonderful with rich venison. These pears can also be served with other full-flavoured barbecued meats, such as pork, pheasant or guinea fowl.

1 Peel the pears, then halve them lengthways and remove the cores with a teaspoon. Brush the flesh with the lemon juice to prevent the pears from discolouring.

2 Combine the wine, juniper berries, lemon rind and cinnamon stick in a saucepan. Bring to the boil, add the pears, cover and simmer gently for 10 minutes or until tender.

3 Using a slotted spoon, transfer the pears to a bowl and set aside. Stir the redcurrant jelly into the liquid remaining in the pan. Boil until reduced by half, pour over the pears and leave to cool.

4 Brush the venison cutlets with a little oil or butter. Cook on an oiled barbecue grill over hot coals for 2–3 minutes on each side. To serve, place 2 cutlets on each plate and add a portion of pears. Garnish with watercress and serve the remaining pears separately.

PREP
20

COOK
25

SERVES
4

rich

4 firm **dessert pears**

2 tablespoons **lemon juice**

300 ml (½ pint) **red wine**

6 **juniper berries**, crushed

pared rind of 1 **lemon**, cut into fine julienne strips

1 **cinnamon stick**

3 tablespoons **redcurrant jelly**

8 **venison cutlets**

oil or melted **butter**, for brushing

watercress, to garnish

125 g (4 oz) drained bottled **artichokes** in oil, 1 tablespoon oil reserved

4 **sun-dried tomatoes** in oil, drained

4 **veal escalopes**, about 125 g (4 oz) each

2 slices of **prosciutto**, cut in half

4 **bocconcini** or 1 ball of **mozzarella cheese** cut into 4 pieces

oil, for brushing

salt and **pepper**

PREP
20

COOK
5

SERVES
4

hearty

Veal escalopes with artichoke paste

These neat little veal parcels are filled with a sweet artichoke and tomato paste, enclosing soft, molten mozzarella. Bocconcini – tiny mozzarella cheeses – are available from delicatessens and supermarkets.

1 Place the artichokes, the reserved oil and sun-dried tomatoes in a food processor or blender and work to a smooth paste. Scrape into a bowl and stir in salt and pepper to taste.

2 Sandwich each veal escalope between 2 sheets of clingfilm and flatten with a rolling pin or meat mallet until they are very thin. Spread each escalope with a quarter of the artichoke paste, top with a half slice of prosciutto and a bocconcini. Fold the veal over to make a neat parcel and seal each end with a presoaked cocktail stick.

3 Brush the parcels with oil. Cook on an oiled barbecue grill over hot coals for about 4–5 minutes, turning frequently.

Rabbit with oyster mushrooms

Rabbit meat is nutritious and low in fat, and cooks very well on the barbecue. If you can't get hold of oyster mushrooms, button mushrooms make a great alternative.

1   To make the marinade, mix the wine, tarragon, olive or hazelnut oil, lemon rind and peppercorns in a large, shallow non-metallic dish. Add the rabbit portions and turn to coat. Cover and marinate for 6–8 hours or overnight in the refrigerator.

2   Beat the butter until light and fluffy, stir in the hazelnuts, then season to taste with salt and pepper. Place a 25 cm (10 inch) square piece of greaseproof paper on a work surface. Spoon the butter evenly down the centre, roll over the paper to form a long thin sausage, then twist the ends and place in the refrigerator to harden.

3   Shortly before cooking the rabbit, thread the mushrooms on to 8 skewers, winding the pancetta between them. Brush with the melted butter.

4   Remove the rabbit pieces from the marinade and cook them on an oiled barbecue grill over hot coals for 20–25 minutes or until tender, turning and basting frequently with the remaining marinade. Add the mushroom skewers to the grill for the final 5 minutes, turning frequently.

5   Place 2 rabbit portions on each plate, add a mushroom skewer and dot with slices of the hazelnut butter. Serve with grilled celery, if liked.

PREP
10*

COOK
25

SERVES
4

nutty

300 ml (½ pint) **dry white wine**

2 tablespoons chopped **tarragon**

3 tablespoons **olive oil** or **hazelnut oil**

strips of rind from 1 **lemon**

1 teaspoon **black peppercorns**

1 **rabbit**, cut into 8 portions

125 g (4 oz) **butter**, slightly softened

50 g (2 oz) **hazelnuts**, toasted and chopped

salt and **pepper**

grilled celery, to serve (optional)

SKEWERED MUSHROOMS:

250 g (8 oz) **oyster mushrooms**, trimmed

8 slices of **pancetta**

25 g (1 oz) **butter**, melted

poultry

1 tablespoon **olive oil**

1 **onion**, chopped

2 **garlic cloves**, crushed

50 g (2 oz) **chestnuts**, roughly chopped

2 tablespoons chopped **thyme**

625 g (1¼ lb) coarsely minced **turkey**

50 g (2 oz) **breadcrumbs**

1 **egg**

1 tablespoon **cranberry sauce**

a little light **olive oil**, for brushing

salt and **pepper**

TO SERVE

125 g (4 oz) **Brie**

4 **burger buns**

4 tablespoons **cranberry sauce**

salad leaves

PREP
15*

COOK
16

SERVES
4

festive

Turkey and chestnut burgers

Turkey is often mixed with cranberries and chestnuts, as the flavours marry well together to make a nutty and fruity combination.

1 Heat the oil in a pan and fry the onion and garlic for 4 minutes or until the onion has softened. Remove from the heat and add the chestnuts and thyme. Set aside to cool.

2 Put the turkey, breadcrumbs, egg and cranberry sauce in a large bowl with the thyme and chestnut mixture. Season with salt and pepper and mix well. Divide the mixture into 4 portions and shape each one into a ball, then flatten slightly into a burger. Cover and chill for 30 minutes.

3 Brush the burgers with a little oil and cook them on an oiled barbecue grill over medium-hot coals for 6 minutes on each side, or until cooked through.

4 Slice the Brie into 4 pieces, place one on each burger and allow them to melt slightly in the heat from the barbecue.

5 To assemble, halve and toast the buns on the barbecue. Fill with the burgers, top with cranberry sauce and serve with salad leaves.

* plus 30 minutes chilling

Chicken and herb crépinettes

These tasty smooth chicken burgers are wrapped in lacy caul fat. This not only bastes the meat and protects it from drying but gives the burgers added flavour. Caul fat is available from good butchers.

1 Place the bread in a bowl, pour over the milk and leave to stand for 10 minutes. Squeeze the bread, discarding the milk, and place in a food processor. Add the chicken and whizz to a smooth paste.

2 Spoon the mixture into a bowl and stir in the egg white, cream, shallots and chopped parsley and thyme. Season with salt and pepper.

3 Divide the mixture into 4 portions and shape each one into a ball, then flatten slightly into a burger. Soak the caul fat in warm water for 5 minutes, then drain and stretch it out on a chopping board. Cut out 4 x 15 cm (6 inch) squares. Place 1–2 sage leaves in the centre of each square and top with a chicken burger. Fold the caul fat over and secure the back of the crépinettes with a cocktail stick. Transfer the crépinettes to a baking sheet, cover and leave to set in the refrigerator.

4 Meanwhile, cut the peaches in half and discard the stones. Chop the flesh finely and place it in a bowl with the onion, chillies and walnut oil. Mix well and season to taste with salt and pepper.

5 Remove the crépinettes from the refrigerator 20–30 minutes before cooking. Cook on an oiled barbecue grill over hot coals for 15–20 minutes, turning often. Serve at once, with the peach relish.

PREP
50*

COOK
20

SERVES
4

tasty

125 g (4 oz) piece of day-old **bread**, crusts removed

300 ml (½ pint) **milk**

500 g (1 lb) boneless, skinless **chicken breasts**, cubed

1 **egg white**

150 ml (¼ pint) **double cream**

2 **shallots**, finely chopped

2 teaspoons chopped **parsley**

2 teaspoons chopped **thyme**

300 g (10 oz) **caul fat**

8–12 **sage leaves**

salt and **pepper**

PEACH RELISH

2–3 ripe **peaches**, skinned

2 tablespoons chopped **red onion**

1–2 **green chillies**, deseeded and chopped

½ tablespoon **walnut oil**

salt and **pepper**

* plus setting

300 g (10 oz) boneless, skinless **chicken breasts**, chopped

300 g (10 oz) boneless, skinless **chicken thighs**, chopped

2 teaspoons **harissa**

1 **red onion**, finely chopped

4 tablespoons chopped **coriander**

50 g (2 oz) **breadcrumbs**

1 **egg yolk**

light **olive oil**, for brushing

salt and **pepper**

SATAY SAUCE

200 ml (7 fl oz) crunchy **peanut butter**

250 ml (8 fl oz) **coconut milk**

2 tablespoons **soy sauce**

1 **red chilli**, finely chopped

2.5 cm (1 inch) piece of fresh **root ginger**, peeled and grated

2 **garlic cloves**, crushed

juice and grated rind of 1 **lime**

2 tablespoons **sweet chilli sauce**

TO SERVE

1 small bunch of **coriander**

1 **lime**, cut into wedges

PREP
20*

COOK
10

SERVES
4

spicy

Chicken satay burgers

This is perfect as a starter for 6 people or as a hot canapé. For a main course, serve with a crusty roll and extra salad.

1 To make the satay sauce, mix together all the ingredients in a small saucepan, bring to the boil and simmer, stirring continuously, for 2 minutes. Remove from the heat and set aside until needed.

2 Mix together all the ingredients for the burgers except the oil. Divide the mixture into 12 portions and shape each one into a ball, then flatten slightly into a burger. Cover and chill for 30 minutes.

3 Brush the burgers with a little oil and cook them on an oiled barbecue grill over medium-hot coals for about 4 minutes on each side, or until completely cooked through.

4 Garnish the burgers with coriander sprigs and wedges of lime and serve accompanied by a bowl of the satay sauce for dipping.

* plus 30 minutes chilling

Teriyaki chicken burgers

The teriyaki marinade can also be served as a dipping sauce; simply double the quantities of the marinade ingredients and serve the extra sauce in a separate bowl.

1 Put the sake, honey, soy sauce, ginger and garlic in a small pan and boil for 2 minutes. Remove from the heat and leave to cool.

2 Slice each chicken breast in half on a slight angle so that you have 8 equal slices. Score each slice a few times with a sharp knife and place in a large, shallow non-metallic dish. Pour over the marinade, season with salt and pepper, then cover and leave to marinate in the refrigerator for 1 hour.

3 Remove the chicken from the marinade, sprinkle with half the sesame seeds and drizzle with the oil. Cook the chicken on an oiled barbecue grill over hot coals for 8 minutes. Turn the chicken, sprinkle with the remaining sesame seeds and cook for a further 8 minutes, basting with the remaining marinade.

4 To assemble, halve and toast the rolls on the barbecue. Place a little cucumber on the base of each one and top with 2 slices of chicken. Mix together the lettuce, spring onion and coriander and divide equally over the chicken slices. Top with the roll tops and serve with Japanese mayonnaise.

PREP
25*

COOK
20

SERVES
4

oriental

75 ml (3 fl oz) **sake**

1 tablespoon clear **honey**

50 ml (2 fl oz) light **soy sauce**

2.5 cm (1 inch) piece of fresh **root ginger**, peeled and finely grated

1 **garlic clove**, finely grated

4 boneless, skinless **chicken breasts**, about 150–175 g (5–6 oz) each

2 tablespoons **sesame seeds**

1 tablespoon **olive oil**, plus extra for greasing

salt and **pepper**

TO SERVE

4 **soft rolls**

¼ **cucumber**, thinly sliced

Cos lettuce, shredded

3 **spring onions**, shredded

2 chopped tablespoons **coriander**

Japanese mayonnaise

500 g (1 lb) coarsely minced **chicken**

2 **garlic cloves**, crushed

1 bunch of **spring onions**, finely chopped

grated rind of 1 **lemon**

50 g (2 oz) **Parmesan cheese**, freshly grated

2 **anchovies**, chopped

8 **streaky bacon** rashers

a little light **olive oil**, for brushing

salt and **pepper**

TO SERVE

4 small **French baguettes**, cut in half lengthways

1 tablespoon **olive oil**

1 small **Cos lettuce**, separated into leaves

Caesar salad dressing

Parmesan cheese shavings

PREP
25*

COOK
10

SERVES
4

classic

Chicken Caesar burgers

You can buy good Caesar dressing these days, so there's no need to make your own if you don't want to. Get the best quality you can, though.

1 Mix together all the ingredients for the burgers, except the bacon and oil, in a bowl and season with salt and pepper. Divide the mixture into 4 and shape each one into a ball, then flatten slightly into burgers. Wrap each one in 2 rashers of bacon then cover and chill in the refrigerator for at least 30 minutes.

2 Brush the burgers with a little oil and cook them on an oiled barbecue grill over medium-hot coals for 5 minutes on each side or until cooked through.

3 To assemble, brush the insides of the baguettes with oil and toast under a hot grill until golden. Top each one with lettuce leaves and drizzle with some dressing. Place a burger on the salad and top with shaved Parmesan.

* plus 30 minutes chilling

Crunchy chicken burgers

Children will love these burgers – but go easy on the mustard and chilli. Instead of the mustard, you could try using some shop-bought pesto sauce.

1 Place each chicken breast between 2 sheets of clingfilm and beat until thin with a meat mallet or rolling pin. Mix together the breadcrumbs, lemon rind, parsley and chilli and sprinkle on a large plate. Spread the mustard over the chicken escalopes then dip them first in the beaten egg and then the breadcrumbs.

2 Cook the chicken on an oiled barbecue grill over medium-hot coals for about 4 minutes on each side. Carefully arrange the cheese slices over the chicken escalopes and allow them to melt slightly in the heat from the barbecue.

3 To assemble, slice open the baps or burger buns and fill with salad leaves, chicken and sliced ham. Serve with a dollop of mayonnaise on the side.

PREP
15

COOK
10

SERVES
4

crunchy

4 **chicken breasts**, about 150–175 g (5–6 oz) each

125 g (4 oz) **breadcrumbs**

grated rind of 1 **lemon**

2 tablespoons chopped **parsley**

1 large **chilli**, deseeded and finely chopped

1 tablespoon **wholegrain mustard**

1 **egg**, beaten

2 tablespoons **olive oil**

25 g (1 oz) **butter**

4 slices of **Jarlsberg** or **Edam cheese**, about 25 g (1 oz) each

TO SERVE

4 **baps** or **burger buns**

125 g (4 oz) mixed **salad leaves**

4 thin slices of **ham**

1 quantity **Mayonnaise** (see page 236)

550 g (1 lb 2 oz) coarsely minced **chicken**

1 **onion**, finely chopped

2 **garlic cloves**, crushed

grated rind of 1 **lime**

3 tablespoons chopped Thai or ordinary **basil**

3 tablespoons **red Thai curry paste**

a little **olive oil**, for brushing

TO SERVE

a little **olive oil**, for stir-frying

4 heads of **bok choi**, sliced lengthways

4 **crusty sesame seed rolls**

6 tablespoons **sweet chilli sauce**

basil leaves, to garnish

PREP
20*

COOK
10

SERVES
4

oriental

Thai chicken burgers with chilli sauce

For a variation, you could also make mini burgers and serve them as party canapés. This recipe would make around 12. Serve with cocktail sticks rather than rolls.

1 Mix together all the ingredients for the burgers except the oil. Divide the mixture into 4 portions and shape each one into a ball, then flatten slightly into a burger. Cover and chill for 30 minutes

2 Brush the burgers with a little oil and cook them on an oiled barbecue grill over medium-hot coals for 5 minutes on each side or until cooked through.

3 Meanwhile, heat the oil in a wok and stir-fry the bok choi for 2 minutes or until just cooked.

4 To assemble, halve and toast the rolls on the barbecue. Put some bok choi on the base of each roll, then add a burger. Drizzle with sweet chilli sauce and garnish with basil leaves. Place the lid on top or to the side and serve.

* plus 30 minutes chilling

Lemon grass chicken burgers

Puréed lemon grass gives this dish a wonderful flavour and is well worth seeking out. It can be bought in jars from Asian supermarkets.

1 Place all the chicken thigh and breast meat in a food processor and whizz until roughly chopped. Add the spring onions, lemon grass, ginger, garlic and coriander then whizz for a further 2 seconds until combined. Divide the mixture into 4 portions and shape each one into a ball, then flatten slightly into a burger. Cover and chill for 30 minutes

2 Put the soy sauce, fish sauce, vinegar, water and sugar in a pan and heat, stirring, until the sugar dissolves, then boil a little until reduced. Brush the mixture over the burgers, then cook them on an oiled barbecue grill over medium-hot coals for 6 minutes on each side, or until cooked through, basting frequently with the remaining sauce.

3 To assemble, halve and toast the rolls on the barbecue. Cover each base with onions, cucumber and herbs, then place a sticky chicken burger on top. Serve with wedges of lime and the lid on the side.

PREP
20*

COOK
15

SERVES
4

mellow

400 g (13 oz) boneless, skinless **chicken thighs**, chopped

200 g (7 oz) boneless, skinless **chicken breasts**, chopped

1 bunch of **spring onions**, finely chopped

2 tablespoons **lemon grass purée**

2.5 cm (1 inch) piece of fresh **root ginger**, peeled and grated

2 **garlic cloves**, crushed

3 tablespoons chopped **coriander**

1 tablespoon dark **soy sauce**

1 tablespoon **fish sauce**

1 tablespoon **rice wine vinegar**

1 tablespoon **water**

2 tablespoons **caster sugar**

TO SERVE

4 **crusty rolls**

4 **spring onions**, shredded

¼ **cucumber**, cut into thin sticks

8 large **basil leaves** or large **mint leaves**

1 small bunch of **coriander**

4 **lime wedges**

* plus 30 minutes chilling

400 g (13 oz) boneless, skinless **chicken thighs**, roughly chopped

200 g (7 oz) boneless, skinless **chicken breasts**, roughly chopped

1 **onion**, finely chopped

2 **garlic cloves**, crushed

3 tablespoons chopped **tarragon**

1 tablespoon **Dijon mustard**

a little light **olive oil**, for frying

MUSHROOM SAUCE

25 g (1 oz) **butter**

250 g (8 oz) mixed **wild mushrooms**, roughly chopped

1 teaspoon **wholegrain mustard**

1 tablespoon **red wine vinegar**

125 g (4 oz) **crème fraîche**

TO SERVE

4 **crusty rolls**

50 g (2 oz) **wild rocket**

PREP
15*

COOK
20

SERVES
4

rustic

Mushroom chicken burgers

This wonderfully tasty burger is really enhanced by the flavour of the wild mushrooms, so don't stint on them. Use more if you think the sauce needs them.

1 Put the chicken thigh and breast meat in a food processor and whizz until roughly chopped. Add the onion, garlic, tarragon and mustard and whizz for a further 2 seconds until combined. Divide the mixture into 4 portions and shape each one into a ball, then flatten slightly into a burger. Cover and chill for 30 minutes.

2 Melt the butter in a frying pan and gently cook the mushrooms for 4–5 minutes until softened. Stir in the mustard, vinegar and crème fraîche and cook for 1–2 minutes or until the sauce is thick enough to coat the back of a spoon. Place the pan on the side of the barbecue to keep warm while you cook the burgers.

3 Brush the burgers with a little oil and cook them on an oiled barbecue grill over medium-hot coals for 6 minutes on each side, or until cooked through.

4 To assemble, halve and toast the rolls on the barbecue, then top each base with rocket followed by a burger. Spoon the wild mushroom sauce over the top and serve with the bun lid on the side.

* plus 30 minutes chilling

Chicken and goats' cheese burgers

Make sure you get goats' cheese with a rind, rather than the packaged soft cheese that's often available. The cheese with a rind has a richer flavour and will melt more pleasingly over the burgers.

1 Place the figs in a roasting dish and drizzle with the olive oil and honey. Season well with salt and pepper and roast in a preheated oven, 200°C (400°F), Gas Mark 6, for 10 minutes until the figs just start to colour.

2 Meanwhile, sandwich each chicken breast between 2 sheets of clingfilm and flatten slightly with a rolling pin or meat mallet. Rub the thyme and garlic into the chicken, season with salt and pepper and wrap with the Parma ham.

3 Brush the chicken breasts with a little oil and cook them on an oiled barbecue grill over medium-hot coals for about 8 minutes on each side, or until cooked through. Top each breast with a slice of goats' cheese and allow it to melt slightly in the heat from the barbecue.

4 To assemble, halve and toast the rolls on the barbecue, top each base with rocket leaves and a chicken breast, then spoon the honey-roasted figs over each burger. Garnish with extra rocket leaves or thyme sprigs and serve the lids on the side.

PREP
15

COOK
17

SERVES
4

moist

4 boneless, skinless **chicken breasts**, about 150–175 g (5–6 oz) each

2 tablespoons chopped **thyme**

2 **garlic cloves**, crushed

4 thin slices of **Parma ham**

a little light **olive oil**, for brushing

150 g (5 oz) **goats' cheese**

salt and **pepper**

HONEY-ROASTED FIGS

6 ripe **figs**, cut into quarters

2 tablespoons **olive oil**

2 tablespoons clear **orange blossom honey**

salt and **pepper**

TO SERVE

4 **crusty caraway seed rolls**

75 g (3 oz) sprigs of **rocket** or **thyme**

2 **garlic cloves**, crushed

2 tablespoons chopped **flat leaf parsley**

1 tablespoon **olive oil**

4 **chicken breasts**, about 150 g (5 oz) each

salt and **pepper**

SAGE AND ONION STUFFING

1 tablespoon light **olive oil**, plus extra for greasing

1 **onion**, finely chopped

4 **pork sausages**

4 tablespoons chopped **sage**

125 g (4 oz) **breadcrumbs**

1 **egg**, beaten

TO SERVE

4 **crusty rolls**

iceberg lettuce, shredded

PREP
25*

COOK
30

SERVES
4

herby

Sage and onion chicken burgers

Sage and onion are natural partners for chicken, and here they make an unusual but wonderfully flavoursome burger.

1 First make the stuffing. Heat the oil in a frying pan and cook the onion for about 4 minutes until soft but not coloured. Remove from the heat and allow to cool slightly. Remove the skins from the sausages and mix the meat with the cooked onion, sage, breadcrumbs and egg. Divide the mixture into 8 equal portions and shape each one into a ball, then flatten slightly into a burger. Cover and chill for 30 minutes.

2 Mix together the garlic, parsley and olive oil and brush over the chicken breasts, then season well with salt and pepper. Brush the chicken breasts with a little oil and cook them on an oiled barbecue grill over medium-hot coals for about 10–12 minutes on each side, or until cooked through, adding the stuffing burgers halfway through the cooking time.

3 To assemble, halve and toast the rolls on the barbecue. Top each base with shredded lettuce then 2 stuffing burgers and a barbecued chicken breast. Serve immediately with the lid on the side.

* plus 30 minutes chilling

Pesto turkey kebabs

The strong flavours of pesto and sun-dried tomatoes make these rolled-up turkey kebabs very popular.

PREP
15

COOK
12

SERVES
4

intense

4 **turkey breast steaks**, about 500 g (1 lb) in total

2 tablespoons **Pesto** (see page 20)

8 slices of **Parma ham**

125 g (4 oz) **sun-dried tomatoes** in oil, drained and finely chopped

1 ball of **mozzarella cheese**, finely diced

1 tablespoon **olive oil**

salt and **pepper**

chopped **parsley**, to garnish

lemon wedges, to serve

1 Sandwich each turkey steak between 2 sheets of clingfilm and flatten slightly with a rolling pin or meat mallet until they are about 1 cm (½ inch) thick.

2 Spread pesto over each thinned turkey steak and lay 2 slices of Parma ham on top of each. Sprinkle the tomatoes and mozzarella evenly over the turkey steaks, then season to taste and roll up each one from the long side.

3 Cut the turkey rolls into 2.5 cm (1 inch) slices. Carefully thread the slices of roll on to 4 metal skewers, dividing them equally among the skewers.

4 Brush the turkey rolls lightly with oil and cook on an oiled barbecue grill over medium coals for 6 minutes on each side, or until cooked through. Garnish with chopped parsley and serve hot with lemon wedges.

4 boneless, skinless **chicken breasts**, about 150–175 g (5–6 oz) each

2 tablespoons finely chopped **rosemary**

2 **garlic cloves**, finely chopped

3 tablespoons **lemon juice**

2 teaspoons **English mustard**

1 tablespoon clear **honey**

2 teaspoons freshly ground black **pepper**

1 tablespoon **olive oil**

salt

mixed leaf salad, to serve

PREP
10*

COOK
10

SERVES
4

rustic

Rosemary chicken skewers

These versatile kebabs can be given a Greek flavour if you substitute the rosemary with chopped thyme leaves and omit the English mustard. Serve with a feta cheese and tomato salad.

1 Lay a chicken breast between 2 sheets of clingfilm, then flatten it slightly with a mallet or rolling pin. Cut the chicken into thick strips. Repeat with the remaining chicken breasts.

2 Put the chicken strips in a large, shallow non-metallic bowl. Add all the remaining ingredients and mix well. Cover and set aside to marinate for 5–10 minutes.

3 Remove the chicken strips from the marinade and thread on to 8 skewers. Cook on an oiled barbecue grill over hot coals for 4–5 minutes on each side, or until the chicken is cooked through. Serve immediately with a mixed leaf salad.

* plus 5–10 minutes
marinating

Chicken satay

PREP
15*

COOK
5

SERVES
4

fragrant

For a change, you can adapt this recipe to make pork satay or king prawn satay, using the same quantity of thin slices of pork or large raw prawns in place of the chicken.

1 To make the marinade, mix together all the ingredients except for the chicken slices in a large, shallow non-metallic dish. Add the chicken and turn to coat thoroughly. Cover and leave to marinate in the refrigerator for at least 4 hours, giving them an occasional stir.

2 Remove the chicken pieces from the marinade and carefully thread them on to skewers, leaving some space at either end. Cook them on an oiled barbecue grill over hot coals for about 5 minutes, turning once, until cooked through.

3 Garnish with chopped raw onion and chunks of cucumber and serve with the satay sauce.

1 teaspoon **ground cinnamon**

1 tablespoon **ground cumin**

1 teaspoon ground black **pepper**

150 ml (¼ pint) **olive oil**

100 ml (3½ fl oz) light **soy sauce**

2 tablespoons **palm sugar** or **light muscovado sugar**

500 g (1 lb) boneless, skinless **chicken breasts**, thinly sliced into 2.5 x 5 cm (1 x 2 inch) slices

Satay Sauce (see page 105), to serve

TO GARNISH

1 **onion**, roughly chopped

cucumber chunks

2 **onions**, roughly chopped

5 cm (2 inch) piece of fresh **root ginger**, peeled and roughly chopped

4 **garlic cloves**, crushed

300 ml (½ pint) **natural yogurt**

2 **red chillies**, deseeded and chopped

1 tablespoon **ground coriander**

2 teaspoons **ground cumin**

1 teaspoon **turmeric**

8 tablespoons **lemon juice**

2 teaspoons **salt**

1.5 kg (3 lb) boneless, skinless **chicken breasts**, cut into 2.5 cm (1 inch) cubes

lemon wedges or **lime wedges**, to garnish

8 **Naan Breads** (see page 204), to serve

PREP
30*

COOK
12

SERVES
8

spicy

Chicken tikka kebabs with naan bread

It is time consuming to make the marinade, but it can be prepared a day in advance and the chicken can be left to marinate overnight in the refrigerator.

1 Combine all the ingredients except the chicken in a blender or food processor and process until smooth, then tip into a large, shallow non-metallic dish. Add the chicken cubes and toss to coat thoroughly. Cover and leave to marinate in the refrigerator for 8 hours or overnight.

2 Remove the chicken from the marinade and thread on to 16 skewers. Cook the kebabs on an oiled barbecue grill over hot coals for 6 minutes on each side, basting frequently with the marinade.

3 While the kebabs are cooking, wrap the naan breads in a foil parcel and heat on the edge of the barbecue grill. Serve the kebabs with the warm naan and garnish with lemon or lime wedges.

* plus 8 hours marinating

Chicken skewers with spicy couscous

PREP 20*

COOK 15

SERVES 8

spicy

This dish was inspired by the flavours of North Africa. The couscous will fill up your guests without taking up space on the barbecue. You could also use large prawns or pieces of vegetable.

1 To make the marinade, mix together the olive oil, garlic, spices and lemon juice in a large, shallow non-metallic dish. Add the chicken strips and turn to coat thoroughly. Cover and leave to marinate in the refrigerator for 2 hours.

2 To prepare the couscous, heat half of the oil in a saucepan and fry the onion, garlic and spices for 5 minutes. Stir in the dried fruits and almonds and remove from the heat.

3 Meanwhile, pour the hot stock over the couscous, cover with a tea towel and leave for 8–10 minutes, until the grains are fluffed up and the liquid absorbed. Stir in the remaining oil and the fruit and nut mixture, add the lemon juice and coriander and season with salt and pepper to taste.

4 While the couscous is standing, remove the chicken from the marinade and thread on to 16 small skewers. Cook the chicken on an oiled barbecue grill over medium coals for 4–5 minutes on each side, until charred and cooked through. Serve with the couscous and garnished with coriander.

4 tablespoons **olive oil**

4 **garlic cloves**, crushed

1 teaspoon **ground cumin**

1 teaspoon **ground turmeric**

1 teaspoon **paprika**

4 teaspoons **lemon juice**

1 kg (2 lb) boneless, skinless **chicken breasts**, cut into long, thin strips

sprigs of **coriander,** to garnish

COUSCOUS

8 tablespoons **olive oil**

2 small **onions**, finely chopped

2 **garlic cloves**, crushed

2 teaspoons each **ground cumin, cinnamon, pepper** and **ginger**

125 g (4 oz) **dried dates**, chopped

125 g (4 oz) **dried apricots**, finely chopped

125 g (4 oz) **blanched almonds**, toasted and chopped

1.2 litres (2 pints) hot **vegetable stock**

375 g (12 oz) **couscous**

2 tablespoons **lemon juice**

4 tablespoons chopped **coriander**

salt and **pepper**

* plus 2 hours marinating

4 tablespoons dark **soy sauce**, plus extra to serve

4 tablespoons **mirin**

2 tablespoons **caster sugar**

4 boneless, skinless **chicken breasts**, about 150–175 g (5–6 oz) each, cut into 2.5 cm (1 inch) cubes

250 g (8 oz) **soba noodles**

sesame oil, to serve

PREP
10*

COOK
6

SERVES
4

easy

Chicken teriyaki with soba noodles

This combination of hot chicken and cold noodles is exquisite. Salmon works very well in this recipe too. Use 4 salmon fillets instead of chicken, and cook whole for 2–3 minutes on each side until just done.

1 To make the marinade, mix together the soy sauce, mirin and sugar in a large, shallow non-metallic dish. Add the chicken cubes and toss to coat. Cover and leave to marinate for 15 minutes.

2 Meanwhile, cook the noodles according to the packet instructions, then drain, refresh in iced water, drain again and chill.

3 Remove the chicken cubes from the marinade and thread on to skewers. Cook the chicken on an oiled barbecue grill over hot coals for 2–3 minutes on each side. Toss the noodles with a little sesame oil and serve with the chicken and extra sesame oil and soy sauce.

* plus 15 minutes
marinating

Chicken yakitori

PREP
15

COOK
8

SERVES
4

tender

The ultimate Japanese fast food, these small morsels of chicken meat and chicken livers, coated in a sweet sticky glaze, are perfect appetizers to serve with beer at a barbecue lunch party.

1 To make the basting sauce, place the sake, the dark and light soy sauces and the sugar in a small saucepan, bring to the boil, then remove from the heat and set aside to cool.

2 Thread the chicken livers on to 8 skewers and the chicken meat on to another 8, adding alternate pieces of green pepper and spring onion to both. Sprinkle with pepper.

3 Cook the skewers on an oiled barbecue grill over medium-hot coals for about 3 minutes on each side, basting frequently with the remaining sauce. The chicken thigh meat will take a total of 5–6 minutes and the chicken livers 4–5 minutes.

4 Serve the skewers immediately, with grated mouli and sliced cucumber.

4 tablespoons **sake**

4 tablespoons dark **soy sauce**

2 tablespoons light **soy sauce**

2 tablespoons **sugar**

250 g (8 oz) **chicken livers**, cut into 1.5 cm (¾ inch) pieces

4 skinless **chicken thighs**, cut into 5 x 1 cm (2 x ⅓ inch) strips

1 **green pepper**, cored, deseeded and cut into 1.5 cm (¾ inch) squares

6 **spring onions**, cut into 1.5 cm (¾ inch) lengths

pepper

TO SERVE

grated **white mouli** (radish)

sliced **cucumber**

2.5 cm (1 inch) piece of fresh **root ginger**, peeled and very finely grated

2 **garlic cloves**, crushed

finely grated rind and juice of 1 **orange**

2 tablespoons **olive oil**

2 tablespoons **honey**

4 boneless, skinless **chicken breasts**, about 150–175 g (5–6 oz) each, cut into 8 long, thin strips each

green salad, to serve

TOASTED CORN SALSA

2 **corn cobs**, husks and threads removed

3 tablespoons **sunflower oil**

4 **spring onions**, chopped

3 tablespoons chopped **coriander**

2 teaspoons **toasted sesame seeds**

1 tablespoon **lime juice**

1 tablespoon light **soy sauce**

1 teaspoon **sesame oil**

salt and **pepper**

COOK
20

SERVES
4

oriental

Honey and orange chicken sticks

The combination of fresh ginger, honey and orange juice give these chicken sticks a delicious flavour.

1 To make the marinade, place the ginger, garlic, orange rind and juice, oil and honey in a large, shallow non-metallic dish. Add the chicken strips and turn to coat thoroughly. Cover and leave to marinate for 1–2 hours.

2 To make the toasted corn salsa, brush the corn cobs with 2 tablespoons of the sunflower oil and cook on an oiled barbecue grill over medium-hot coals for 10–15 minutes, turning frequently, until the cobs are charred and the kernels are tender. Remove the cobs from the heat and, when cool enough to handle, scrape the kernels from the cobs with a knife.

3 Place the kernels in a bowl, add the remaining oil, the spring onions, coriander, sesame seeds, lime juice, soy sauce and sesame oil and season to taste. Set aside.

4 Remove the chicken strips from the marinade and thread on to 16 skewers, 2 pieces to each skewer. Cook the skewers on an oiled barbecue grill over medium-hot coals for 2–3 minutes on each side until cooked through, basting with any remaining marinade. Serve with the toasted corn salsa and a green salad.

* plus 1–2 hours marinating

Chicken on lemon grass skewers

The flavour of the lemon grass is released as the skewers cook, infusing an incredible perfume and subtle spice into the chicken.

1 Put all the ingredients except the lemon grass in a bowl. Season well, then use your hands to pound and press the mixture together until thoroughly blended. Cover and chill for 10 minutes.

2 Divide the mixture into 8 portions. Mould a portion of mixture on to the end of a lemon grass stalk, forming a sausage shape. Repeat with the remaining portions of mixture and lemon grass.

3 Cook the skewers on an oiled barbecue grill over medium-hot coals for 5–6 minutes on each side or until cooked through. Serve hot, with boiled rice and a mixed salad.

PREP
15*

COOK
12

SERVES
4

subtle

300 g (10 oz) minced **chicken**

1 **garlic clove**, crushed

1 teaspoon grated fresh **root ginger**

1 tablespoon **Thai fish sauce**

2 teaspoons **ground cumin**

2 teaspoons **ground coriander**

1 tablespoon finely chopped **coriander**

1 **red chilli**, deseeded and finely chopped

1 teaspoon **sugar**

grated rind and juice of 1 **lime**

1 tablespoon **desiccated coconut**

8 **lemon grass stalks**

salt and **pepper**

TO SERVE

boiled rice

mixed salad

4 **duck breasts**, about 200–250 g (7–8 oz) each

4 tablespoons **maple syrup**

1 teaspoon **vanilla essence**

juice and finely grated rind of 1 **orange**

juice and finely grated rind of 1 **lime**

curly endive, to serve

APRICOT PECAN CHUTNEY

250 g (8 oz) **dried apricots**

1 large **onion**, sliced

50 g (2 oz) **raisins**

50 g (2 oz) **brown sugar**

300 ml (½ pint) **cider vinegar**

1 teaspoon **yellow mustard seeds**

¼ teaspoon **ground ginger**

¼ teaspoon **cayenne**

1 tablespoon **salt**

50 g (2 oz) shelled **pecan nuts**, chopped

PREP
30

COOK
55

SERVES
4

spicy

Maple duck with apricot pecan chutney

Sweet, tender duck skewers with a piquant chutney make a perfect partnership and an unusual barbecue dish.

1 To make the apricot pecan chutney, place all the ingredients, except the pecans, in a heavy-based saucepan or preserving pan. Bring to a boil, then reduce the heat to very low and simmer very gently for 45 minutes or until thick. Stir frequently to prevent sticking. Stir in the pecans and pour into sterilized jars while still hot. Cover and seal.

2 Using a sharp knife, cut away any excess fat and score the skin of the duck in a criss-cross pattern. Cut the breasts into 3.5 cm (1½ inch) cubes and thread on to the skewers. In a small bowl, mix together the maple syrup, vanilla essence, fruit juice and rind.

3 Cook the skewers on an oiled barbecue grill over medium-hot coals for 2 minutes on each side. Remove from the heat and brush with the glaze. Return the duck to the barbecue and continue cooking for 5–8 minutes until cooked through, turning and basting frequently with any remaining marinade. Serve immediately with some of the chutney on a bed of curly endive.

Tandoori chicken

COOK
30

Vary this classic Indian recipe by using 750 g (1½ lb) cubed shoulder of lamb instead of the chicken. It's sure to be a winner, whatever meat you use.

SERVES
4

1 Put the chilli, garlic, ginger and lemon juice in an electric spice mill or food processor with the whole spices and garam masala, then work to a smooth paste.

2 Transfer the spice paste to a large, shallow non-metallic dish. Add the yogurt, food colouring and salt and stir well to mix. Set aside.

classic

3 Score the flesh of the chicken deeply with a sharp-pointed knife, cutting right down as far as the bone. Put the chicken in a single layer in the dish, then spoon the marinade over the chicken and work it into the cuts in the flesh. Cover and marinate in the refrigerator for at least 4 hours, but preferably overnight.

4 Cook the chicken on an oiled barbecue rack over hot coals, turning frequently, for 30 minutes or until the juices run clear when pierced with a skewer or fork. Serve hot, garnished with lemon wedges and coriander sprigs.

1 hot **red chilli**, deseeded and roughly chopped

2 **garlic cloves**, roughly chopped

2.5 cm (1 inch) piece of fresh **root ginger**, roughly chopped

2 tablespoons **lemon juice**

1 tablespoon **coriander seeds**

1 tablespoon **cumin seeds**

2 teaspoons **garam masala**

6 tablespoons **natural yogurt**

few drops each of red and yellow **food colouring**

4 skinless **chicken breasts**, about 150–175 g (5–6 oz) each

salt

TO GARNISH

lemon wedges

sprigs of **coriander**

100 ml (3½ fl oz) **sweet sherry**

1 teaspoon **Angostura bitters**

1 tablespoon light **soy sauce**

1 tablespoon chopped fresh **root ginger**

pinch of **ground cumin**

pinch of **ground coriander**

1 teaspoon **dried mixed herbs**

1 small **onion**, finely chopped

75 ml (3 fl oz) **chicken stock**

4 boneless, skinless **chicken breasts**, about 150 g (5 oz) each

salt and **pepper**

sprigs of **flat leaf parsley**, to garnish

PREP
10*

COOK
20

SERVES
4

spicy

Carnival chicken

Children love this fragrant chicken, so it makes a great barbie dish for all the family.

1 To make the marinade, mix together all the ingredients except the chicken in a large, shallow non-metallic dish. Add the chicken breasts and turn to coat thoroughly. Cover and leave to marinate in the refrigerator overnight.

2 Remove the chicken from the marinade and cook on an oiled barbecue grill over medium-hot coals for 10 minutes on each side. Season with salt and pepper and serve, garnished with parsley.

* plus overnight
marinating

South-east Asian grilled chicken

Like many of the best barbecue recipes, this one comes from South-east Asia. Steamed mixed rice makes a good accompaniment to this dish.

PREP
30*

COOK
30

SERVES
4

Thai

1 Cut 3 diagonal slits in each chicken breast and place in a large, shallow non-metallic dish.

2 Place all the remaining ingredients in a food processor or blender and purée until smooth. Pour the marinade over the chicken and turn to coat thoroughly. Cover and leave the chicken to marinate for 1–1½ hours.

3 Meanwhile, to make the pineapple and peanut relish, mix all the ingredients in a bowl, cover and set aside.

4 Remove the chicken breasts from the marinade and cook on an oiled barbecue grill over hot coals for 25–30 minutes, or until tender and cooked through.

5 Transfer the chicken to individual plates, garnish with lime wedges and serve with the pineapple and peanut relish.

4 **chicken breasts**, about 150–175 g (5–6 oz) each

2 **lemon grass stalks**, finely chopped

juice of 2 **limes**

2 **red chillies**, deseeded and chopped

3 **garlic cloves**, crushed

2.5 cm (1 inch) piece of fresh **root ginger**, finely chopped

2 tablespoons **soft dark brown sugar**

2 tablespoons chopped **coriander**

150 ml (¼ pint) **coconut milk**

lime wedges, to garnish

PINEAPPLE AND
PEANUT RELISH

1 small **pineapple**, peeled, cored and finely chopped

1 **red onion**, chopped

3 tablespoons **lime juice**

1 **garlic clove**, crushed

1 tablespoon light **soy sauce**

25 g (1 oz) **roasted unsalted peanuts**, chopped

4 boneless **chicken breasts**, about 175–250 g (6–8 oz) each

125 g (4 oz) **soft goats' cheese**

25 g (1 oz) **walnuts**, finely chopped

2 tablespoons chopped **flat leaf parsley**

2 tablespoons **Dijon mustard**

3 tablespoons **olive oil**

1 **garlic clove**, crushed

salt and **pepper**

young leaf spinach, to serve

TOMATO AND CHIVE VINAIGRETTE

15 g (½ oz) **chives**, chopped

100 ml (3½ fl oz) **extra virgin olive oil**

juice and finely grated rind of 1 **lime**

500 g (1 lb) ripe **tomatoes**, skinned (see page 13), deseeded and chopped

salt and **pepper**

PREP
20*

COOK
20

SERVES
4

tasty

* plus 30 minutes chilling

Chicken stuffed with goats' cheese

This summery dish with its refreshing vinaigrette is always a popular choice at a barbecue.

1 Pull away the small fillets from the flesh of the chicken breasts, place in between 2 pieces of clingfilm and flatten gently with a rolling pin or mallet. Set aside. Place each chicken breast skin side down, insert a small knife into the thickest part of the flesh and slice along to create a pocket.

2 To make the stuffing, mix the goats' cheese, walnuts and parsley and season to taste. Divide the mixture into 4 and spoon a quarter into each chicken pocket. Place the small chicken fillet over the slit and draw the edges of the chicken breast around it. Place the chicken breasts on a tray, cover and leave to rest in the refrigerator for 30 minutes.

3 To make the tomato and chive vinaigrette, place the chives in a food processor or blender with the oil and process until smooth. Pour into a small bowl and stir in the lime juice and rind. Season with salt and pepper and gently stir in the chopped tomatoes.

4 Mix the mustard, olive oil and garlic. Brush the chicken breasts with this glaze, then cook, skin side down, on an oiled barbecue grill for 15–20 minutes, turning once and basting occasionally with the remaining glaze.

5 Serve the chicken on a bed of fresh young leaf spinach, with the vinaigrette sprinkled around.

Duck breasts with olives and oranges

Duck skin is very fatty, but salting the duck before cooking it in this way draws out any excess moisture and makes the skin deliciously crisp.

PREP
15*

COOK
30

SERVES
4

sweet

4 **duck breasts**, about 250 g (8 oz) each

250 g (8 oz) coarse **sea salt**

4 **oranges**

2 pieces of **stem ginger** in syrup, drained and chopped

125 g (4 oz) **black olives**

15 g (½ oz) **butter**

pepper

1 Place one duck breast, skin side up, on a large double piece of foil, sprinkle with half of the salt and top with a second duck breast, skin side down. Wrap tightly in foil. Repeat with the remaining pair of duck breasts. Chill both parcels for at least 12 hours, preferably 24–36 hours.

2 To prepare the caramelized mixture, finely grate the rind of 2 of the oranges, then peel and segment all 4, working over a bowl to catch any juices. Place the segments in the bowl and mix in the orange rind, ginger and olives. Place this mixture on a large doubled piece of foil with the edges turned up (or use an aluminium tray), and dot with the butter. Cook the open parcel on an oiled barbecue grill over hot coals for about 25–30 minutes, tossing the mixture every now and then, until the oranges are slightly caramelized.

3 Meanwhile, separate the duck breasts, rinse them well and pat dry on kitchen paper. Season with pepper and cook them on the oiled barbecue grill over hot coals, skin side down for the first 5 minutes then turn and seal the other side. Continue cooking the duck alongside the parcel of olives and oranges for 10–15 minutes, turning occasionally, until the duck skin is crisp and the flesh tender but still pink. Serve with the olive and orange mixture.

* plus 12–36 hours salting

1 **pomegranate**

2 **shallots**, chopped

1 teaspoon **pink peppercorns** bottled in brine, drained and crushed

8 **wood pigeon breasts**

1 tablespoon **sugar**

125 g (4 oz) **raspberries**

melted **butter**, for brushing

1 **radicchio**, separated into leaves

1 bunch of **watercress** or **rocket**

50 g (2 oz) **walnuts**, chopped

PREP
20*

COOK
10

SERVES
4

special

Pink pigeon breast salad

A pretty salad of warm pigeon breasts with pink peppercorns, pomegranate seeds and raspberries – a stunning starter for a smart barbecue party.

1 Break open the pomegranate and remove the seeds, discarding the bitter yellow pith. Set aside a quarter of the seeds for the sauce and place the rest in a food processor or blender. Process for just long enough to release the juice, then strain through a fine sieve into a shallow bowl. Add the shallots and pink peppercorns. Mix well, then add the pigeon breasts and toss to coat. Cover the dish and marinate for 1–2 hours.

2 Remove the pigeon breasts from the marinade and set aside. Pour the marinade into a saucepan, stir in the sugar, bring to the boil and cook until reduced by half. Add the raspberries and reserved pomegranate seeds, remove the pan from the heat immediately and set the sauce aside while you cook the pigeon breasts.

3 Brush the pigeon breasts with a little melted butter. Place on an oiled barbecue grill over hot coals and sear quickly on both sides for 1–2 minutes. Remove the breasts from the heat and slice thinly.

4 Arrange the radicchio and watercress or rocket on 4 plates. Top with the pigeon breasts, spoon over the sauce and sprinkle with the chopped walnuts. Serve at once.

* plus 1–2 hours
marinating

Lemon and herb chicken wings

Use the same mixture to coat chicken drumsticks or thighs, or try turkey portions instead.

PREP
5

COOK
20

SERVES
4

herby

1 Put the garlic, lemon rind and juice, thyme leaves, oil, honey, oregano and cumin in a large, shallow non-metallic dish, and season to taste with salt and pepper. Add the chicken wings and stir until well coated.

2 Cook the chicken wings on an oiled barbecue grill over medium-hot coals for 15–20 minutes, turning and basting until they are charred and cooked through.

2 **garlic cloves**, crushed

grated rind and juice of 1 **lemon**

4 sprigs of **thyme**

6 tablespoons **olive oil**

1 tablespoon clear **honey**

1 teaspoon **dried oregano**

1 teaspoon **ground cumin**

12 **chicken wings**

salt and **pepper**

2 **garlic cloves**

8 cm (3 inch) piece of fresh **root ginger**, peeled and chopped

juice and finely grated rind of 4 **limes** or 2 **lemons**

4 tablespoons light **soy sauce**

4 tablespoons **groundnut oil**

4 teaspoons **ground cinnamon**

2 teaspoons **ground turmeric**

4 tablespoons **honey**

16 large **chicken wings**

salt

sprigs of **coriander**, to garnish

YELLOW PEPPER DIP

4 **yellow peppers**, deseeded and cut into quarters

8 tablespoons **natural yogurt**

2 tablespoons dark **soy sauce**

2 tablespoons chopped **coriander**

pepper

PREP
30*

COOK
18

SERVES
8

spicy

Cinnamon-spiced chicken wings

Unusual, sweet and spicy, this is a delicious way to serve chicken wings. Because they are quite small, you can get lots of wings on the barbie at a time.

1 To make the marinade, put all the ingredients except for the chicken in a blender or food processor and process until very smooth, then pour into a large, shallow non-metallic dish. Add the chicken and turn to coat thoroughly. Cover and leave to marinate for 2–3 hours.

2 To make the yellow pepper dip, grill the pepper quarters, skin side down, on an oiled barbecue grill over hot coals for 6–8 minutes until charred and tender. Put into a plastic bag, seal and set aside until cool enough to handle. Peel off the skin, put the flesh in a food processor or blender with the yogurt and whizz until smooth. Pour into a bowl, add the soy sauce and season with pepper to taste; stir in the chopped coriander and set aside.

3 Remove the chicken from the marinade and cook on an oiled barbecue grill over medium-hot coals for 4–5 minutes on each side, basting with the remaining marinade. Garnish with coriander and serve with the dip.

Jamaican jerk chicken

PREP
15*

COOK
20

SERVES
4–6

hot

Jerk seasoning can be used with other cuts of chicken, such as thighs or breasts. It is also very good with pork.

1 Put all the ingredients except for the chicken drumsticks in a food processor or spice mill and grind to a paste.

2 Score the chicken drumsticks deeply with a sharp-pointed knife, cutting right down as far as the bone.

3 Put the chicken in a large, shallow non-metallic dish and coat with the jerk seasoning mixture, brushing it into the slashes in the meat so that the flavour will penetrate. Cover and marinate in the refrigerator overnight.

4 Cook the drumsticks on an oiled barbecue grill over hot coals for about 20 minutes, turning frequently, until the chicken is charred on the outside and no longer pink on the inside. Serve hot, warm or cold.

2 tablespoons **rapeseed oil**

1 small **onion**, finely chopped

10 **allspice berries**

2 hot **red chillies**, deseeded and roughly chopped

3 tablespoons **lime juice**

1 teaspoon **salt**

12 **chicken drumsticks**

* plus overnight marinating

5 cm (2 inch) piece of fresh **galangal** or **root ginger**, peeled and finely chopped

4 **garlic cloves**, crushed

1 large **red chilli**, finely chopped

4 **shallots**, finely chopped

2 tablespoons finely chopped **coriander leaves**

150 ml (¼ pint) thick **coconut milk**

1.5 kg (3 lb) **chicken**, spatchcocked (see page 13)

salt and **pepper**

TO SERVE

sweet chilli sauce, for dipping

lime wedges

PREP
20*

COOK
40

SERVES
4–6

spicy

Thai barbecued chicken

You can spatchcock the chicken and put it into the marinade the night before, so it just needs to be put on the barbecue when you come home after a busy day at work.

1 Put the galangal or ginger, garlic, red chilli, shallots and coriander in a food processor and whiz to a paste; alternatively, use a pestle and mortar. Add the coconut milk and mix until well blended.

2 Rub the chicken all over with salt and pepper and place in a large, shallow non-metallic dish. Pour the coconut marinade over the chicken, making sure it is coated thoroughly. Cover and leave to marinate in the refrigerator overnight.

3 Remove the chicken from the marinade and cook it on an oiled barbecue grill over medium-hot coals for 30–40 minutes, turning and basting regularly with the remaining marinade, until the juices run clear when the thickest part of a thigh is pierced with a fork.

4 Leave the chicken to stand for 5 minutes, then chop it into small pieces. Serve with sweet chilli dipping sauce and lime wedges.

* plus overnight marinating

Spatchcocked poussins

PREP
25

COOK
20

SERVES
4

moist

Spatchcocking is a term used for splitting and flattening a bird for cooking. The method is ideal for barbecuing as it speeds up the cooking process and cooks the meat evenly.

1 Place the sun-dried tomatoes in a food processor or blender, add the butter and basil and season with salt and pepper, then purée until smooth. Transfer the paste to a bowl. Alternatively, chop the tomatoes and basil finely and beat with the butter in a bowl. Cover and chill.

2 Lift the skin covering each poussin breast and gently push your fingers between the flesh and skin to make a pocket. Divide the sun-dried tomato and basil butter equally among the poussins, pushing it underneath the skin.

3 Working with one bird at a time, thread a skewer through a drumstick, under the breastbone and through the second drumstick. Thread another skewer through the wings, catching the flap of skin underneath. (This helps to flatten the bird so that it can cook evenly.)

4 Brush the poussins with the reserved oil from the tomatoes, place on a oiled barbecue grill and cook over medium-hot coals for 15–20 minutes until the juices run clear when the thickest part of a thigh is pierced with a fork. Suitable accompaniments would be a chicory and frisée salad, and a vegetable such as grilled, sliced fennel.

3 **sun-dried tomatoes** in oil, drained and chopped, with oil reserved

125 g (4 oz) **butter**, softened

3 tablespoons roughly chopped **basil**

4 **poussins**, about 500 g (1 lb) each, spatchcocked (see page 13)

salt and **pepper**

chicory and **frisée salad** and/or **grilled, sliced fennel**, to serve

1–1.5 kg (2–3 lb) **guinea fowl**, spatchcocked (see page 13)

butter or **oil**, for brushing

MUSHROOM STUFFING

25 g (1 oz) **dried porcini mushrooms**, soaked for 30 minutes in warm water to cover

50 g (2 oz) **butter**

2 **shallots**, finely chopped

1 **garlic clove**, crushed

250 g (8 oz) **field mushrooms**, finely chopped

2 tablespoons chopped **parsley**

salt and **pepper**

PREP
30

COOK
50

SERVES
4

tasty

Guinea fowl with porcini stuffing

The mushroom stuffing provides a moist and tasty filling for these spatchcocked guinea fowl, which make an impressive centrepiece for a barbecue.

1 To make the stuffing, drain the mushrooms through a sieve lined with kitchen paper set over a bowl. Reserve the liquid. Rinse the mushrooms under cold water, drain again, then chop finely.

2 Melt the butter in a saucepan. Add the shallots and garlic and cook gently for 2–3 minutes until soft but not coloured. Add both types of mushrooms and cook for 4–5 minutes more. Stir in the reserved mushroom liquid and boil hard until all the liquid has evaporated. Off the heat, stir in the parsley and add salt and pepper to taste. Cool slightly.

3 Lift and loosen the skin on the guinea fowl gently, easing it away from the breast and leg meat with your fingers. Take care not to make any holes. Spoon the stuffing under the skin and spread it out evenly. Pull the skin back tightly over the bird and secure underneath with a skewer or cocktail sticks.

4 Brush the guinea fowl with a little butter or oil. Cook breast side down on an oiled barbecue grill over hot coals for 10–15 minutes. Turn the bird over and cook for 10–15 minutes more. Continue cooking, turning the bird occasionally, until the juices run clear when the thickest part of a thigh is pierced with a fork. Transfer to a platter, leave to rest for a few minutes, then carve.

Partridges with port and grape sauce

Serve this sophisticated dish at a smart barbecue to impress your guests.

PREP
15

COOK
25

SERVES
4

stylish

1 Stuff each partridge with an onion quarter and a strip of lemon rind. Place 2 strips of pancetta or bacon across the breast of each one and tie with string. Mix the butter, parsley, salt and pepper, and spread some over each bird.

2 Place a drip tray on the hot coals of a barbecue and place an oiled grill rack on the setting nearest the coals. Sear the birds for 2–3 minutes on each side, then raise the rack to a position 10–12 cm (4–5 inches) from the coals and cook for a further 12–15 minutes, turning frequently, until the birds are tender and the juices run clear when the thickest part of the thigh is pierced.

3 Transfer the birds to a heated platter, ignite the ladle of warmed brandy and pour it over the birds. Make a tent of foil over the birds to keep them hot.

4 Pour the juices from the drip tray into a saucepan. Add the juniper berries, port, redcurrant jelly and the grapes. Bring to the boil and reduce for 2–3 minutes. Skim the surface, then pour the sauce into a bowl and serve with the partridges.

4 oven-ready **partridges**, about 375 g (12 oz) each,

1 **onion**, quartered

4 strips of **lemon rind**

4 slices of **pancetta** or rindless **streaky bacon**, halved lengthways

50 g (2 oz) **butter**, slightly softened

1 tablespoon chopped **parsley**

4 tablespoons **brandy**, warmed in a ladle

salt and **pepper**

PORT AND GRAPE SAUCE

6 **juniper berries**, crushed

50 ml (2 fl oz) **port**

3 tablespoons **redcurrant jelly**

500 g (1 lb) **black grapes**, cut in half lengthways and deseeded

fish

3 **shallots**, thinly sliced

2.5 cm (1 inch) piece of fresh **root ginger**, grated

1 **garlic clove**, crushed

1 tablespoon clear **honey**

4 tablespoons **Japanese soy sauce**

2 tablespoons **rice wine vinegar**

4 **tuna steaks**, about 200 g (7 oz) each

2 tablespoons **olive oil**

WASABI MAYO

8 tablespoons **Mayonnaise** (see page 236)

1–2 teaspoons **wasabi**

TO SERVE

4 **burger buns**

¼ **cucumber**, shredded

frisée leaves

8 large **mint leaves**, shredded

PREP
10*

COOK
8

SERVES
4

fiery

Tuna steaks with wasabi mayonnaise

Wasabi is a Japanese horseradish with a sharp, fiery and pungent flavour. You can buy it in dried and paste form from most Asian stores.

1 To make the wasabi mayonnaise, simply mix together the two ingredients and chill until needed.

2 To make the marinade, mix the shallots, ginger, garlic, honey, soy sauce and vinegar in a large, shallow non-metallic dish. Add the tuna and turn to coat. Cover and leave to marinate for 1 hour (but no longer or the vinegar in the marinade will start to 'cook' the fish).

3 Remove the tuna steaks from the marinade and cook them on an oiled barbecue grill over medium-hot coals for 3–4 minutes on each side, basting frequently with the remaining marinade.

4 To assemble, halve and toast the buns on the barbecue, fill them with some shredded cucumber, frisée and mint and a tuna steak, and serve with a dollop of wasabi mayo on the side.

* plus 1 hour marinating

Tuna Niçoise

PREP
20*

COOK
20

SERVES
4

classic

If you can't find quails' eggs, use 4 hens' eggs instead, and boil them for 5–8 minutes.

1 Put the quails' eggs in a pan of boiling water; lower the heat and simmer for 3 minutes. Refresh under cold running water, then shell the eggs.

2 Boil the potatoes in lightly salted water for 10 minutes until just tender. Drain, refresh under cold running water and drain again.

3 Blanch the French beans in a separate saucepan of boiling water for 3–4 minutes. Tip into a colander, refresh under cold water and drain again. Place the eggs and vegetables in separate bowls and set aside until required. Do not chill.

4 To make the marinade, mix together the olive oil, parsley, lemon juice and peppercorns in a large, shallow non-metallic dish. Add the tuna steaks in a single layer and turn to coat thoroughly. Cover and leave to marinate for 30–60 minutes, turning once.

5 Remove the tuna from the marinade and cook on an oiled barbecue grill over hot coals for 3–4 minutes on each side, until just cooked, basting frequently with the remaining marinade.

6 Meanwhile, combine the potatoes, beans, olives, tomatoes, anchovies and lettuce in a large bowl. Mix the dressing ingredients. Pour the dressing over the bowl of salad and toss lightly. Top with the eggs and hot tuna and serve with plenty of crusty bread.

12 **quails' eggs**

500 g (1 lb) **baby new potatoes**

250 g (8 oz) fine **French beans**, topped and tailed

6 tablespoons **olive oil**

2 tablespoons chopped **parsley**

½ tablespoon **lemon juice**

2 tablespoons mixed whole **peppercorns**, crushed

4 **tuna steaks**, about 175 g (6 oz) each

125 g (4 oz) **black olives**, pitted

4 ripe **tomatoes**, quartered

12 canned **anchovy fillets**, drained

1 **Cos lettuce**

crusty bread, to serve

DRESSING

1 **garlic clove**, crushed

1 tablespoon **white wine vinegar**

5 tablespoons **olive oil**

* plus 30–60 minutes marinating

4 thick **tuna steaks**, about 250 g (8 oz) each

12 **anchovies** in oil, drained and cut in half

4 **garlic cloves**, cut into thin slivers

2 tablespoons **olive oil**

salt and **pepper**

crisp **green salad**, to serve

CAPER VINAIGRETTE

100 ml (3½ fl oz) **extra virgin olive oil**

2 tablespoons **white wine vinegar**

1 teaspoon **Dijon mustard**

1 tablespoon chopped **tarragon**

1 tablespoon chopped **flat leaf parsley**

2 tablespoons **capers**, rinsed and drained

pinch of **sugar**

salt and **pepper**

PREP
15

COOK
8

SERVES
4

tasty

Tuna with caper vinaigrette

Note that tuna should be only just cooked or it becomes tough. If you like your tuna rare, cook the steaks for just 2 minutes on each side.

1 To make the caper vinaigrette, whisk the olive oil, vinegar and mustard in a small bowl. Stir in the tarragon, parsley and capers and season with salt, pepper and a pinch of sugar. Cover and set aside.

2 With a small sharp knife, make 6 small incisions in each tuna steak. Using the end of the knife, poke a piece of anchovy fillet and a sliver of garlic into each incision.

3 Brush all the steaks with olive oil and season with salt and pepper. Place the steaks on an oiled barbecue grill and cook over medium-hot coals for 3–4 minutes on each side until just cooked. Serve with the caper vinaigrette and a crisp green salad.

Tahini tuna with noodles and pak choi

Tahini paste is made from sesame seeds; it has a mild nutty flavour and is also often used as an ingredient in hummus.

1 Season the tuna steaks with salt and coarsely ground pepper and coat with olive oil. Cook on an oiled barbecue grill over hot coals for 3–4 minutes on one side. Carefully turn the tuna steaks over and spread the top of each steak with some of the tahini paste. Cook for a further 3–4 minutes.

2 Meanwhile, bring a saucepan of water to the boil, add the soba noodles and pak choi and simmer for 5 minutes or until the noodles are just cooked. Also, place the sesame seeds in a frying pan and dry-fry for a few minutes until golden, stirring frequently.

3 Mix the soy sauce, rice wine vinegar and honey in a jug. Drain the noodles and pak choi and pour the soy mixture over them both and toss together. Put a mound of noodles and pak choi on each plate and top with the tuna. Sprinkle with the toasted sesame seeds and serve with lemon or lime wedges.

PREP
10

COOK
10

SERVES
4

nutty

4 **tuna steaks**, about 250 g (8 oz) each

1 tablespoon **olive oil**

4 tablespoons **tahini paste**

250 g (8 oz) **soba noodles**

4 baby **pak choi**

1 teaspoon **sesame seeds**

6 tablespoons **soy sauce**

4 tablespoons **rice wine vinegar**

2 teaspoons clear **honey**

sea salt and **pepper**

lemon wedges or **lime wedges**, to serve

250 g (8 oz) **rice noodles**

1½ tablespoons **sesame oil**

1½ tablespoons **sesame seeds**, toasted, plus
1 tablespoon for garnish

2 tablespoons **lime juice**

5 tablespoons **groundnut oil**

2 **garlic cloves**, crushed

4 **tuna steaks**, about 250 g (8 oz) each, skinned

4 tablespoons **dried pink peppercorns**, crushed

salt

PICKLED GINGER

6 tablespoons **rice vinegar**

1 tablespoon **sugar**

1 teaspoon **salt**

50 g (2 oz) **piece of fresh root ginger**, peeled and cut into wafer-thin slices

PREP
25*

COOK
4

SERVES
8

peppery

Peppered tuna with pickled ginger

To cook tuna like the Japanese takes only a minute: the outside of the fish should be seared while the inside remains pink and moist.

1 To prepare the pickled ginger, place the rice vinegar, sugar and salt in a small saucepan. Bring to the boil, add the sliced ginger, lower the heat and simmer for about 1–2 minutes. Remove from the heat, transfer to a bowl and leave to cool.

2 Prepare the noodles according to the packet instructions. Drain and refresh under cold water, then drain again. Tip the noodles into a bowl, add the sesame oil and sesame seeds and toss lightly.

3 To make the marinade, combine the lime juice, groundnut oil, garlic and salt to taste in a large, shallow non-metallic dish. Add the fish in a single layer, toss lightly until coated, then cover the dish and marinate the tuna for 1 hour, turning once.

4 Place the peppercorns on a plate. Drain the tuna, discarding the marinade. Roll the edges of each tuna steak in the peppercorns, then sprinkle them with a little salt.

5 Cook on an oiled barbecue grill over moderately hot coals for 1 minute on each side to sear the edges. Slice thinly and serve with the ginger and noodles, sprinkled with sesame seeds to garnish.

* plus 1 hour marinating

Grilled sardines with chilli oil

PREP
15*

COOK
18

SERVES
4

fresh

125 ml (4 fl oz) **olive oil**

2 tablespoons chopped **dried red chillies**

12 small **sardines**, cleaned and scaled

coarse **sea salt**

TO SERVE

lemon wedges

crusty bread

tomato and onion salad

To save time, you can buy chilli oil, but it tends to be hot. Mix just a few drops of bought chilli oil with 125 ml (4 fl oz) of olive oil.

1 Place the oil and chillies in a small pan. Heat very gently for about 10 minutes. Remove from the heat, cover and leave to cool and infuse for 8–12 hours or overnight.

2 Strain the flavoured oil through a sieve lined with muslin or a clean tea towel, then pour it into a sterilized jar or bottle.

3 Brush the sardines with a little of the chilli oil, sprinkle with coarse sea salt and cook on an oiled barbecue grill over hot coals for 6–8 minutes, or until just cooked, turning once. Serve immediately, with lemon wedges, crusty bread and a tomato and onion salad.

* plus 8–12 hours infusing

1 kg (2 lb) sharp **red plums**, pitted and cut into wedges

50 g (2 oz) **sugar**

2 teaspoons **coriander seeds**, crushed

2 **garlic cloves**, crushed

pinch of **paprika**

2 teaspoons finely grated **lemon rind**

8 tablespoons **water**

8 whole **mackerel**, about 375 g (12 oz) each

salt and **pepper**

PREP
25

COOK
15

SERVES
8

tasty

Grilled mackerel with plum sauce

This pretty plum sauce is perfect with mackerel, providing a slightly acidic counterpoint to the oiliness of the fish.

1 Put the plums in a saucepan with the sugar, coriander seeds, garlic, paprika, lemon rind and water. Bring to the boil, cover, lower the heat and simmer gently for about 10 minutes until softened.

2 Spoon the plum mixture into a food processor or blender and purée until smooth. Strain through a sieve into a clean pan, bring to the boil and cook for 5 minutes until thickened and reduced, stirring constantly to prevent the sauce from burning.

3 Meanwhile, cut 3 diagonal slashes on both sides of each fish. Season and cook on an oiled barbecue grill over hot coals for 6–7 minutes on each side.

4 Place the freshly grilled mackerel on individual plates. Pour the hot, thick plum sauce into a bowl and serve immediately with the grilled fish.

Spicy fish satay

Mango or pineapple would be a good alternative to the papaya. The sweetness of the fruit is delicious with the chilli.

1   To make the marinade, mix together the garlic, ginger, soy sauce, lime or lemon juice and chilli in a large, shallow non-metallic dish. Add the mackerel pieces and turn to coat well. Cover and leave to marinate for 30–60 minutes.

2   To make the satay sauce, heat the oil in a small saucepan. Add the garlic and shallot and cook for 3–4 minutes until lightly golden. Pour in the measurement water, sugar, chilli powder and peanuts, stir well and bring to a boil, reduce the heat and simmer, stirring occasionally, for 10–15 minutes or until the sauce has thickened. Remove from the heat and stir in the lime or lemon juice and season with salt and pepper.

3   Remove the fish from the marinade and thread 3 pieces on to each skewer, adding a piece of papaya to the end of each one.

4   Cook the skewers on an oiled barbecue grill over medium-hot coals for 3–4 minutes on each side. Serve with the warm satay sauce

1 **garlic clove**, crushed

2.5 cm (1 inch) piece of fresh **root ginger**, chopped and crushed in a garlic press

2 teaspoons light **soy sauce**

1 tablespoon **lime** or **lemon juice**

1 small **red chilli**, very finely chopped

500 g (1 lb) **mackerel fillets**, each cut into 2.5 cm (1 inch) diagonal strips

½ **papaya**, peeled, deseeded and cut into chunks

SATAY SAUCE

2 tablespoons **sunflower** or **groundnut oil**

1 large **garlic clove**, crushed

1 **shallot**, finely chopped

400 ml (14 fl oz) **water**

1 tablespoon **dark brown sugar**

½ teaspoon **chilli powder**

125 g (4 oz) **unsalted roasted peanuts**, finely ground

1 tablespoon **lime juice** or **lemon juice**

salt and **pepper**

4 **salmon fillets**, about 200 g (7 oz) each

1 tablespoon prepared **English mustard**

1 teaspoon grated fresh **root ginger**

1 teaspoon crushed **garlic**

2 teaspoons clear **honey**

1 tablespoon light **soy sauce**

salt and **pepper**

LIME COURGETTES

2 tablespoons **olive oil**

500 g (1 lb) **courgettes**, thinly sliced lengthways

grated rind and juice of 1 **lime**

2 tablespoons chopped **mint**

salt and **pepper**

PREP
5*

COOK
15

SERVES
4

minty

Chargrilled mustard salmon

A tasty light lunch that is both healthy and delicious. The lime courgettes are so easy to prepare and are guaranteed to impress.

1 To make the marinade, mix together all the ingredients except for the salmon in a large, shallow non-metallic dish. Add the salmon fillets, skin side down, in a single layer and turn to coat thoroughly. Cover and leave to marinate overnight in the refrigerator.

2 Remove the salmon fillets from the marinade and cook on an oiled barbecue grill over medium-hot coals for 10–15 minutes, depending on their thickness, until they are lightly charred and cooked through.

3 Meanwhile, brush the courgette slices with oil and cook on the barbecue grill for 2–3 minutes on each side, then drizzle with the lime juice and rind, mint and seasoning. Serve hot with the salmon.

* plus overnight marinating

Salmon and samphire parcels

Samphire is combined with rich salmon and a nutty pistachio and basil butter in a foil parcel.

PREP
15

COOK
20

SERVES
4

unusual

1   To make the pistachio and basil butter, place the butter, pistachios, basil, garlic and lime juice in a food processor or blender. Add salt and pepper to taste and blend until the sauce is smooth and green. Spoon the mixture into a small bowl, cover and chill in the refrigerator.

2   Place each salmon fillet on a double piece of foil large enough to enclose it completely. Top each fillet with a quarter of the samphire and add a generous tablespoon of the pistachio and basil butter. Bring up the edges of the foil and press together to seal each parcel.

3   Cook the salmon parcels on an oiled barbecue grill for 15–20 minutes over medium coals. Just before serving, carefully open one of the parcels and check that the fish is cooked: it should flake easily when tested with a knife but still be moist. Serve with Hasselback potatoes.

4 **salmon fillets**, about 200 g (7 oz) each

150 g (5 oz) **samphire**

Hasselback Potatoes, to serve (see page 187)

PISTACHIO AND BASIL BUTTER

125 g (4 oz) **butter**, slightly softened

50 g (2 oz) shelled, **unsalted pistachio nuts**

2 tablespoons chopped **basil**

1 **garlic clove**, crushed

1–2 teaspoons **lime juice**

salt and **pepper**

500 g (1 lb) **salmon fillets**, skinned

4 **spring onions**, finely chopped

1 **courgette**, roughly grated

50 g (2 oz) **breadcrumbs**

1 **egg yolk**

a little **oil**, for brushing

PEA SALSA

200 g (7 oz) frozen **peas**

½ **red onion**, finely chopped

3 tablespoons chopped **mint**

juice of 1 **lime**

2 tablespoons **olive oil**

TO SERVE

4 **crusty rolls**

50 g (2 oz) **baby spinach leaves**

1 **beef tomato**, sliced

PREP
20*

COOK
6–10

SERVES
4

light

Salmon burgers with pea salsa

An easy after-work dinner for all the family – children will particularly love the salsa and it is a great way to encourage them to eat vegetables.

1 To make the salsa, put the peas in a pan of boiling water, bring back to the boil, then drain and refresh under cold running water. Tip into a food processor and process until finely chopped, then pour into a bowl and stir in the rest of the salsa ingredients. Set aside.

2 Blitz the salmon fillet in a food processor or blender until finely chopped. Add all the remaining burger ingredients except the oil and process until just mixed but not puréed. With slightly wet hands, divide the mixture into 4 portions and shape each one into a ball, then flatten slightly into a burger. Cover and chill for 30 minutes.

3 Brush the burgers with a little oil and cook them on an oiled barbecue grill over medium-hot coals for about 3–4 minutes on each side, until cooked through.

4 To assemble, halve and toast the rolls on the barbecue, then top each base with some baby spinach, tomato slices and a burger. Top each burger with some minted pea salsa and serve with the lid on the side.

* plus 30 minutes chilling

Sesame salmon fillets

PREP
10

COOK
8

SERVES
4

simple

The black sesame seeds give a real professional restaurant look to this burger; you can buy them in most Japanese or Indian stores.

1 Spread the sesame seeds on a large plate, then dip in the salmon fillets so the top side of each fillet is evenly coated.

2 Cook the salmon on an oiled barbecue grill over medium-hot coals for about 4 minutes on each side until cooked through. Remove from the heat and drizzle over the roasted sesame oil.

3 To assemble, halve and toast the rolls on the barbecue, fill with some cucumber and red onion and a salmon burger and serve immediately.

8 tablespoons **sesame seeds**

4 tablespoons **black sesame seeds**

4 **salmon fillets**, about 150 g (5 oz) each, skinned

1 tablespoon **roasted sesame oil**

TO SERVE

2 **crusty sesame seed rolls**

½ **cucumber**, cut into ribbons with a vegetable peeler

1 small **red onion**, finely sliced

mixed **salad leaves**, to serve

1 whole **fish**, about 1.5 kg (3 lb), cleaned and scaled

1 tablespoon **lime juice** mixed with 1 teaspoon **salt**

1 small **onion**, roughly chopped

1 **red** or **yellow pepper**, cored, deseeded and roughly chopped

2.5 cm (1 inch) piece of fresh **root ginger**, peeled and roughly chopped

2 **garlic cloves**, roughly chopped

2 **red chillies**, deseeded and roughly chopped

1 **lemon grass stalk**, chopped

125 ml (4 fl oz) **coconut milk**

½ teaspoon **chilli powder**

15 g (½ oz) **coriander**

banana leaves, for wrapping (optional)

PREP
20

COOK
20–30

SERVES
4

tender

Whole baked fish in banana leaves

This recipe can be made with many different sorts of fish. Try parrot fish, snapper or red sea bream.

1 Cut 2–3 diagonal slits in each side of the fish. Rub the slits with the lime juice and salt, cover the fish and set aside.

2 Place all the remaining ingredients, except the wrapping, in a food processor or blender and process until smooth. Scrape the paste into a bowl.

3 Put the banana leaves, if using, in a bowl and pour boiling water over them, then drain; this makes them easier to bend and wrap. Lay the fish on top of the leaves. Rub a quarter of the paste into the fish, turn the fish over and rub in another quarter of the mixture. Wrap the leaves securely around the fish, making sure that there are no holes in the parcel; tie with string. Alternatively, wrap the fish in a double thickness of foil.

4 Cook the wrapped fish on an oiled barbecue grill over medium-hot coals for 10–15 minutes on each side, until the flesh is tender. Transfer the parcel to a large platter and turn back the leaves or foil to reveal the fish. Heat the remaining paste in a small saucepan and serve with the fish.

Stuffed rainbow trout

PREP
20

COOK
25

SERVES
4

tasty

Pretty, gleaming, iridescent trout are delicious when served with a simple lemony stuffing and a creamy horseradish sauce.

1 To make the horseradish sauce, put all the ingredients in a food processor or blender and process until smooth. Scrape into a bowl and season to taste with salt and pepper.

2 Melt 125 g (4 oz) of the butter in a small pan, add the chopped almonds, breadcrumbs, lemon rind and juice, and salt and pepper. Mix together well, then stuff the mixture into the trout cavities and reshape the fish.

3 Brush 4 large double pieces of foil with the remaining butter, lay a trout on each and wrap up tightly. Cook on an oiled barbecue grill over medium-hot coals for 20–25 minutes, or until the fish comes away from the bone, turning once. Serve immediately with the sauce.

150 g (5 oz) **butter**

125 g (4 oz) **blanched almonds**, toasted and chopped

125 g (4 oz) **white breadcrumbs**

juice and finely grated rind of 1 **lemon**

4 **rainbow trout**, about 375 g (12 oz) each, cleaned

salt and **pepper**

HORSERADISH SAUCE

125 ml (4 fl oz) **soured cream**

4 teaspoons grated **horseradish**

4 tablespoons chopped **parsley**

2 tablespoons chopped **mint**

salt and **pepper**

4 large unpeeled **potatoes**, thinly sliced

4 tablespoons **olive oil**

4 **sea bass fillets**, about 200 g (7 oz) each

salt and **pepper**

LIME AÏOLI

4–6 **garlic cloves**, crushed

2 **egg yolks**

juice and finely grated rind of 2 **limes**

300 ml (½ pint) **extra virgin olive oil**

salt and **pepper**

PREP
15

COOK
10

SERVES
4

classic

Sea bass with lime aïoli

Allow the sea bass skin to cook until it is crisp before turning over the fillets – the crispy skin is quite delicious to eat.

1 First make the aïoli. Place the garlic and egg yolks in a food processor or blender, add the lime juice and process briefly to mix. With the machine running, gradually add the olive oil in a thin, steady stream until the mixture forms a thick cream. Turn into a bowl, stir in the lime rind and season to taste. Set aside.

2 Brush the potato slices well with olive oil and sprinkle with salt and pepper. Cook them on an oiled barbecue grill over medium-hot coals for 2–3 minutes on each side, or until tender and golden. Remove from the heat and keep warm while you cook the fish.

3 Score the sea bass fillets, brush well with the remaining olive oil and place on the barbecue grill, skin side down. Cook for 3–4 minutes until just cooked, turning once. Remove from the heat and serve with the potatoes and lime aïoli.

Swordfish with almond and herb pesto

Serve this herb and nut pesto with any barbecued fish. You can also vary the flavours by using basil or coriander instead of the parsley.

1 To make the pesto, spread the almonds on a baking sheet and place it under a preheated grill for 2–3 minutes, turning the almonds often until they are toasted and golden. (You may have to break one open to see.)

2 Place half of the toasted almonds in a food processor or blender with all the remaining pesto ingredients and process until smooth, scraping down the sides of the bowl if necessary. Roughly chop the remaining almonds and stir into the pesto.

3 Brush the swordfish steaks with olive oil and cook over hot coals for 2–3 minutes on each side, or until just cooked through. Season with salt and pepper and serve the fish with the pesto, garnished with lemon wedges.

PREP
10

COOK
10

SERVES
4

herby

4 **swordfish steaks**, about 175 g (6 oz) each

olive oil, for brushing

salt and **pepper**

lemon wedges, to garnish

ALMOND AND HERB PESTO

125 g (4 oz) whole **unblanched almonds**

1 **garlic clove**, crushed

2 tablespoons finely grated **Parmesan cheese**

50 g (2 oz) **parsley**, roughly chopped

200 ml (7 fl oz) **extra virgin olive oil**

2 tablespoons **ricotta cheese**

salt and **pepper**

100 g (3½ oz) **butter**, softened

2 tablespoons finely snipped **chives**

1 tablespoon prepared **English mustard**

4 **swordfish steaks** or **fillets**, about 200 g (7 oz) each

4 tablespoons **lemon juice**

salt and **pepper**

TO GARNISH

whole chives

lemon wedges

TO SERVE

cherry tomato salad

boiled rice or **new potatoes**

PREP
5*

COOK
8

SERVES
4

hearty

Swordfish and mustard and chive butter

Mahi mahi and halibut are particularly good in place of the swordfish as they are also firm and flavoursome.

1 In a small bowl, mix the butter, chives and mustard. Turn the butter out on to a piece of greaseproof paper and press it into a sausage shape. Wrap the paper around the butter, twist the ends and roll the butter into a neat sausage, then chill it in the freezer for 10–15 minutes or until firm.

2 Put the swordfish on an oiled grill rack over hot coals, sprinkle with lemon juice and season well. Cook for 6–8 minutes or until cooked through, when the fish will flake easily.

3 While the fish is grilling, remove the butter from the freezer and cut it into slices. Transfer the fish to warmed serving plates and top with the butter. Garnish with chives and lemon wedges and serve immediately with a cherry tomato salad and boiled rice or new potatoes.

* plus 10–15 minutes chilling

Sizzling fish in banana leaves

This delicious Vietnamese dish can also be made with large king prawns or chicken fillets instead of the fish.

PREP
20

COOK
10

SERVES
4

hot

1 **lemon grass stalk**, very finely chopped

2 large **garlic cloves**, finely chopped

1 **kaffir lime leaf**, finely shredded

2 **shallots**, finely chopped

125 g (4 oz) **butter**

2 teaspoons **lime juice**

1 tablespoon finely chopped **coriander**

1 **green chilli**, finely chopped

1 **red chilli**, finely chopped

4 large squares of **banana leaf**

4 **swordfish**, **snapper** or **sea bass fillets**, 2.5 cm (1 inch) thick

salt and **pepper**

1 Blend the lemon grass, garlic, lime leaf and shallots to a smooth paste in a food processor or with a pestle and mortar. Add the butter, lime juice, coriander, chillies, salt and pepper and blend again.

2 Put the banana leaves in a bowl and pour boiling water over them, then drain; this makes them easier to bend and wrap. Place a fish fillet in the centre of each leaf and cover it with some of the lemon grass mixture. Wrap it tightly and secure with a presoaked bamboo skewer or cocktail stick. Alternatively, you can wrap the fish in a double thickness of foil.

3 Chill the fish parcels until needed or put them straight on an oiled barbecue grill and cook over medium-hot coals for 8–10 minutes, turning once. Place the fish wrapped in the banana leaves on individual plates. Cut open the parcels and serve the fish immediately.

4 **swordfish steaks**, about 175 g (6 oz) each

2 tablespoons **olive oil**

BLACK OLIVE BUTTER

125 g (4 oz) **unsalted butter**, softened

25 g (1 oz) pitted **black olives**, very finely chopped

½ teaspoon **anchovy paste**

1 **garlic clove**, crushed

1 tablespoon **capers**, finely chopped

juice and finely grated rind of ½ **lemon**

salt and **pepper**

PREP
15*

COOK
8

SERVES
4

simple

Swordfish with black olive butter

The black olives add a taste of the Mediterranean to this simple, yet tasty, dish.

1 To make the black olive butter, beat together all the ingredients until well combined.

2 Arrange a long piece of greaseproof paper on a work surface and spread the butter down the middle. Roll the paper over and twist the ends until you have a neat sausage. Chill in the refrigerator until firm.

3 Brush the swordfish steaks with the olive oil and cook on an oiled barbecue grill over medium-hot coals for 3–4 minutes on each side until just cooked. Unroll the black olive butter and cut it into slices. Serve each steak with a slice of butter.

* plus chilling

Swordfish steak burgers

PREP
20

COOK
10

SERVES
4

fruity

It is the salsa that steals the show in this recipe – fresh, citrussy and spicy, it can also be served with chicken dishes.

1 To make the salsa, mix together the orange, parsley, chilli and spring onions in a bowl. Heat the oil in a frying pan and cook the garlic, ginger and cumin seeds until crisp. Tip the contents of the pan into the orange mixture and stir. Set aside until needed.

2 Mix together the spices, orange rind and oil, season with salt and pepper and rub over both sides of the swordfish steaks.

3 Cook the steaks on an oiled barbecue grill over medium-hot coals for 8–10 minutes, turning once, until cooked through.

4 To assemble, halve and toast the rolls on the barbecue, then fill with salad leaves and the fish steaks and spoon over the orange salsa.

1 teaspoon **ground cumin**

1 teaspoon **ground coriander**

1 teaspoon **paprika**

pinch of **ground chilli**

grated rind of 1 **orange**

2 tablespoons **olive oil**

4 **swordfish steaks**, about 175 g (6 oz) each

salt and **pepper**

CRUNCHY ORANGE SALSA

1 large **orange**, segmented and finely chopped

3 tablespoons finely chopped **flat leaf parsley**

1 **red chilli**, finely chopped

3 **spring onions**, finely chopped

3 tablespoons **olive oil**

3 **garlic cloves**, finely sliced

2.5 cm (1 inch) piece of fresh **root ginger**, peeled and cut into fine matchsticks

1 teaspoon **cumin seeds**

TO SERVE

4 **crusty sesame seed rolls**

mixed **salad leaves**

4 boneless firm **white fish fillets** such as John Dory, cod or sole, about 175 g (6 oz) each

2 tablespoons **olive oil**, plus extra for oiling

50 g (2 oz) **polenta**

salt and **pepper**

crisp **salad**, to serve

LEMON AND SESAME MAYONNAISE

1 **egg yolk**

2 tablespoons **lemon juice**

½ teaspoon **Dijon mustard**

150 ml (5 fl oz) **sunflower oil**

1 teaspoon **sesame oil**

finely grated rind of 1 small **lemon**

salt and **pepper**

PREP
15

COOK
6

SERVES
4

crunchy

Polenta-crusted fish

The polenta gives the fish fillets a crisp, crunchy coating. Served with a simple mayonnaise and a fresh green salad, what could be nicer?

1 To make the mayonnaise, place the egg yolk, lemon juice and mustard in a food processor and process until amalgamated. Mix the sunflower and sesame oil together and, with the motor running, gradually add the oils in a thin, steady stream. When the mayonnaise is thick, stir in the lemon rind and season to taste. Transfer to a bowl, cover and set aside.

2 Brush the fish fillets all over with the olive oil. Arrange the fillets on a plate flesh side up and sprinkle liberally with the polenta, then season with salt and pepper.

3 Heat a metal griddle on the barbecue and, when hot enough, oil well. (Alternatively lay a piece of heavy-duty foil on the barbecue grill.) Lay the fish fillets on the griddle and cook for 3 minutes on each side until just cooked. Serve the fillets immediately with a crisp salad and the lemon and sesame mayonnaise.

Nutty cod with banana and coconut salsa

This recipe gives you a little taste of the Caribbean in your own home. The lime juice in the salsa will stop the banana from turning brown.

PREP 20*

COOK 6

SERVES 4

funky

1   Mix together the ground peanuts, chilli powder, crushed allspice and salt and sprinkle on a large plate. Dip each cod fillet into the melted butter and then into the peanut mixture, shaking off any excess. Cover and set aside.

2   If using desiccated coconut, place in a bowl with warm water to cover. Leave to soak for 20 minutes, then strain through a sieve, pressing the coconut against the sides with the back of a spoon to squeeze out any excess moisture.

3   To make the banana salsa, mix together the crushed garlic, lime rind and juice, red onion, coriander and coconut. Just before serving, chop the banana into small dice and gently stir into the salsa mixture.

4   Heat a metal griddle on the barbecue and, when hot enough, oil well. (Alternatively lay a piece of heavy-duty foil on the barbecue grill.) Place the cod fillets on the griddle and cook for 4–6 minutes until just done, turning once. Serve immediately with the banana and coconut salsa.

75 g (3 oz) **unsalted roasted peanuts**, finely chopped

¼ teaspoon **chilli powder**

6 **allspice berries**, finely crushed

½ teaspoon **salt**

4 **cod fillets**, about 175–250 g (6–8 oz) each

75 g (3 oz) **butter**, melted

a little light **olive oil**, for oiling

BANANA AND COCONUT SALSA

75 g (3 oz) grated **fresh coconut** or 25 g (1 oz) unsweetened **desiccated coconut**

1 small **garlic clove**, crushed

finely grated rind and juice of 1 **lime**

½ small **red onion**, finely chopped

2 tablespoons chopped **coriander**

3 **bananas**

* plus 20 minutes soaking, if using desiccated coconut

1 **egg**

1 teaspoon **English mustard powder**

75 g (3 oz) **breadcrumbs**

2 tablespoons finely chopped **basil**

25 g (1 oz) **Parmesan cheese**, freshly grated

4 tablespoons **plain flour**

4 **cod fillets**, about 175 g (6 oz) each

2 tablespoons light **olive oil**

salt and **pepper**

TO SERVE

4 **crusty poppy seed rolls**

mixed **salad leaves**

1 **beef tomato**, sliced

4 tablespoons **Lemon Mayonnaise** (see page 239)

lemon wedges

PREP
15

COOK
6

SERVES
4

simple

Parmesan-crusted cod burgers

The lemon mayonnaise provides a tangy contrast to the Parmesan-coated fish fillets in this simple but succulent recipe.

1 First make the crust for the fish. Beat the egg and mustard with a little salt and pepper. Mix together the breadcrumbs, basil and Parmesan in a bowl, then tip on to a plate. Spread the flour on a separate plate.

2 Coat the cod fillets in the flour and dip them first in the egg mixture then coat them evenly in the breadcrumb mixture.

3 Heat a metal griddle on the barbecue and, when hot enough, oil well. (Alternatively, lay a piece of heavy-duty foil on the barbecue grill.) Place the cod fillets on the griddle and cook for 4–6 minutes until just done, turning once.

4 Halve and toast the rolls on the barbecue, fill them with the salad leaves, tomato slices and crusted cod fillets and serve with lemon mayonnaise, lemon wedges and extra salad.

Cajun fish burgers

PREP
15*

COOK
10

SERVES
4

spicy

Tabasco sauce is very hot and peppery, all you will need are a few drops – too much will mask the flavour of the fish and can make it unpalatable.

1 Heat a small frying pan and add all the ingredients for the Cajun spice mix; cook for 1 minute until the spices start to smoke slightly. This will enhance their flavours. Set aside to cool.

2 Skin and bone the fish fillets, then chop them roughly. Put them in a food processor with the breadcrumbs, onion, garlic, egg, Tabasco and spice mix and process until thoroughly blended and the mixture holds together. Don't overblend, as you want the fish to retain some texture.

3 With slightly wet hands, divide the mixture into 4 equal portions; shape them into balls, then flatten into burgers. Cover and chill for 1 hour.

4 Cook the burgers on an oiled barbecue grill over medium-hot coals for 5 minutes on each side, or until cooked through.

5 To assemble, halve and toast the rolls on the barbecue, then fill with some salad and a burger.

625 g (1¼ lb) **white fish fillets**

50 g (2 oz) **breadcrumbs**

1 small **onion**, grated

1 **garlic clove**

1 **egg yolk**

1 teaspoon **Tabasco sauce**

CAJUN SPICE MIX

3 teaspoons **paprika**

1 teaspoon **cayenne pepper**

1 teaspoon **dried thyme**

1 teaspoon **dried parsley**

1 teaspoon **dried oregano**

½ teaspoon **onion salt**

a pinch of **cinnamon**

TO SERVE

4 **crusty rolls**

salad leaves

500 g (1 lb) ripe **tomatoes**, skinned (see page 13)

1 tablespoon **balsamic vinegar**

2 **monkfish fillets**, about 375 g (12 oz) each, skinned

4 **garlic cloves**, cut into thin slivers

2 long **rosemary sprigs**

5 tablespoons **olive oil**

1 tablespoon **lemon juice**

salt and **pepper**

crusty bread, to serve

PREP
20*

COOK
20

SERVES
4

herby

Monkfish with garlic and rosemary

Rosemary is a very powerful herb. Here the monkfish fillets are tied together with rosemary sprigs, so the aroma permeates the fish without being overwhelming.

1 Place the tomatoes in a food processor or blender and process until smooth. Strain through a sieve into a bowl, season to taste with the vinegar, salt and pepper, then cover and set aside.

2 Slice each monkfish fillet lengthways, almost but not quite all the way through, to make a pocket. Lay the garlic slivers down the length of the pocket in each fillet and top with a rosemary sprig. Add salt and pepper to taste. Reform both fillets and tie them with string at 1.5 cm (¾ inch) intervals.

3 To make the marinade, mix together the olive oil and lemon juice in a large, shallow non-metallic dish. Add the monkfish and turn to coat thoroughly. Cover and leave to marinate for 1 hour.

4 Drain the monkfish and cook on an oiled barbecue grill over medium-hot coals for 15–20 minutes, basting frequently, until the flesh is opaque and just cooked. Meanwhile, pour the tomato sauce into a small saucepan and heat through. Remove the string and slice the fish thinly. Serve with the tomato sauce and some good crusty bread.

* plus 1 hour marinating

Seafood brochettes

Monkfish and sweet scallops, lightly chargrilled outside and soft and tender inside, are served with a creamy golden mayonnaise.

1 To make the saffron mayonnaise, place the saffron threads in a small bowl. Pour over the boiling water and leave to infuse for 10 minutes. Combine the egg yolks and lemon juice in a separate bowl. Add the saffron and its soaking liquid and whisk the mixture until slightly thickened. Continue to whisk briskly, gradually adding the oil in a thin, steady stream until the mixture forms a thick, creamy mayonnaise. Taste and adjust the seasoning if required.

2 To make the marinade, mix the lime juice, oil and seasoning in a large, shallow non-metallic dish. Add the cubes of monkfish and the prepared scallops and toss to coat thoroughly. Cover and leave to marinate in the refrigerator for 30 minutes.

3 Remove the fish and scallops from the marinade and thread alternately on to 8 skewers. Cook on an oiled barbecue grill over medium-hot coals for about 3–4 minutes, turning frequently and basting with the remaining marinade. Serve immediately with the saffron mayonnaise.

PREP
25*

COOK
4

SERVES
4

tender

2 teaspoons **lime juice**

3 tablespoons **sunflower oil**

salt and **pepper**

375 g (12 oz) **monkfish fillets**, skinned and cut into 2.5 cm (1 inch) cubes

12 **scallops**, cut in half crossways if large

SAFFRON MAYONNAISE

pinch of **saffron threads**

1 tablespoon boiling **water**

2 **egg yolks**

1 tablespoon **lemon juice**

200 ml (7 fl oz) **sunflower oil**

salt and **pepper**

4 **dried fennel stalks**, about 20 cm (8 inches) long

2 tablespoons **olive oil**

1 **garlic clove**, crushed

8 large **scallops**

500 g (1 lb) **monkfish fillets**, cut into 12 large chunks

salt and **pepper**

bread, to serve

FENNEL SAUCE

3 tablespoons chopped **fennel** or **dill**

pinch of **dried chilli flakes**

2 teaspoons **lemon juice**

6–8 tablespoons **olive oil**

1 **fennel bulb**

salt and **pepper**

PREP
15*

COOK
6

SERVES
4

delicate

Scallop and monkfish skewers

Dried fennel stalks make good skewers as they are rigid and impart their mild aniseed flavour into the food during cooking.

1 Pull off the dried leaves still attached to the fennel stalks, leaving a clump at one end, and soak the stalks in cold water for at least 30 minutes.

2 To make the marinade, mix together the olive oil, garlic and some pepper in a large, shallow non-metallic dish. Cut away the tough white muscle from each scallop and remove any intestine. Wash and pat dry and add to the marinade with the monkfish cubes. Toss to coat thoroughly. Cover and leave to marinate for at least 30 minutes.

3 Meanwhile, make the fennel sauce. Mix together the fennel or dill, chilli flakes, lemon juice and oil, and season with salt and pepper to taste. Cover and set aside to infuse. Just before serving, thinly slice the fennel bulb and toss with the sauce.

4 Remove the seafood from the marinade and thread on to the fennel stalks. Season the seafood with salt and cook on an oiled barbecue grill over hot coals for 5–6 minutes, turning once and basting with the marinade, until charred and tender. Serve the skewers hot, with the fennel sauce and some bread to mop up the juices.

* plus 30 minutes soaking and 30 minutes marinating

Stuffed baby squid

PREP
40

COOK
4

SERVES
4

tasty

Perfect for the barbecue, these sweet-tasting baby squid are filled with a colourful Mediterranean-inspired stuffing.

1 Chop the squid tentacles finely, then place them in a mixing bowl. Add the olives, capers, garlic, tomatoes, oregano, breadcrumbs and lemon juice; stir in 4 tablespoons of the olive oil and mix well.

2 Use this mixture to stuff the squid. Secure the open end of each one with a presoaked cocktail stick and brush the squid lightly with oil.

3 Cook the stuffed squid on an oiled barbecue grill over medium-hot coals for about 3–4 minutes, turning frequently, until just cooked. Serve the squid immediately.

500 g (1 lb) **baby squid**, cleaned and prepared

50 g (2 oz) **black olives**, pitted and chopped

2 tablespoons bottled **capers**, drained and chopped

1–2 **garlic cloves**, crushed

4 **tomatoes**, skinned (see page 13), deseeded and chopped

4 tablespoons chopped **oregano**

125 g (4 oz) **white breadcrumbs**

1½ tablespoons **lemon juice**

4 tablespoons **olive oil**, plus extra for brushing

3 tablespoons chopped **oregano**

5 tablespoons **olive oil**

2 **shallots**, finely chopped

1 tablespoon **lemon juice**

375 g (12 oz) **baby squid**, cleaned and prepared

12 large raw **prawns** in their shells

RED PEPPER SAUCE

2 **red peppers**, deseeded and cut into quarters

2 **red chillies**

1 tablespoon **sherry vinegar**

salt and **pepper**

PREP
20*

COOK
25

SERVES
4

smoky

Barbecued squid and prawns

When barbecued, the flavour of squid and fresh prawns can be fully appreciated. This cooking method gives a smoky, sweet, chargrilled taste, which perfectly complements the hot peppery sauce.

1 To prepare the sauce, grill the pepper quarters, skin side down, and the chillies on an oiled barbecue grill over hot coals for 6–8 minutes for the peppers, and 3–4 for the chillies, until charred and tender. Put them all into a plastic bag, seal and set aside until cool enough to handle. Peel off the skin, deseed the chillies and slice the flesh, then pat dry with kitchen paper.

2 Put the peppers and chillies in a food processor or blender, add the sherry vinegar and process until smooth. Season to taste with salt and pepper.

3 To make the marinade, mix the oregano, olive oil, shallots and lemon juice in a large, shallow non-metallic dish. Cut the squid flesh into 2.5 cm (1 inch) squares and score the squares in a criss-cross pattern. Add the squid and prawns to the marinade and toss to coat thoroughly. Cover and marinate for 30–40 minutes.

4 Remove the seafood from the marinade and thread on to skewers. Cook the kebabs on an oiled barbecue grill over moderately hot coals for 6–8 minutes, turning once and basting frequently with the remaining marinade. Place the kebabs in deep soup bowls and pour the sauce over the top.

* plus 30–40 minutes marinating

Coconut butterflied prawns

This spicy coconut marinade works equally well on scallops or cubes of monkfish or chicken.

1 To butterfly the prawns, hold a prawn with the back uppermost and slice along its length, from the thickest part towards the tail, cutting it almost but not quite through. Gently press the prawn to flatten it out and make the butterfly shape. Repeat with the remaining prawns, then rinse them well under cold running water.

2 To make the marinade, mix the garlic, ginger, lime juice, chillies and coconut cream in a large, shallow non-metallic dish. Pat the prawns dry on kitchen paper, add them to the marinade and turn to coat thoroughly. Cover and marinate for 1–2 hours.

3 Drain the prawns and thread them on to 4 skewers. Cook on an oiled barbecue grill over medium-hot coals for 5–6 minutes, turning once, until the flesh is opaque and just cooked. Serve the skewers immediately.

PREP
10*

COOK
6

SERVES
4

spicy

12 large raw **tiger prawns**, peeled, but tails retained, and deveined

2 **garlic cloves**, crushed

1 cm (½ inch) piece of fresh **root ginger**, peeled and very finely shredded

2 tablespoons **lime juice**

1–2 **red chillies**, deseeded and finely chopped

150 ml (¼ pint) **coconut cream**

* plus 1–2 hours marinating

4 tablespoons **olive oil**

2 **garlic cloves**, finely crushed

1 teaspoon **ground cumin**

½ teaspoon **ground ginger**

1 teaspoon **paprika**

¼ teaspoon **cayenne pepper**

1 bunch of **coriander**, finely chopped

500 g (1 lb) large raw **tiger prawns**, peeled, but tails retained, and deveined

salt

lemon wedges, to serve

PREP
10*

COOK
6

SERVES
4

spicy

Mediterranean prawns

Tiger prawns are delicious, if expensive, making this simple dish an absolute delight. These prawns can also be butterflied for a more exotic appearance (see page 127).

1 To make the marinade, mix together all the ingredients except for the prawns in a large, shallow non-metallic dish. Add the prawns and toss to coat thoroughly. Cover and leave to marinate for 30 minutes.

2 Remove the prawns from the marinade and thread on to 4 skewers. Cook on an oiled barbecue grill over medium-hot coals for 2–3 minutes on each side. Serve hot, accompanied by lemon wedges.

* plus 30 minutes
marinating

Prawn and mango kebabs

PREP
10*

COOK
4

SERVES
4

hot

These pretty kebabs are quite spicy, so reduce the amount of chilli powder if you prefer milder food.

1 To make the marinade, put all the ingredients except for the prawns and mango in a large, shallow non-metallic dish. Add the prawns and toss to coat thoroughly. Cover and leave to marinate for about 10 minutes.

2 Remove the prawns from the marinade and thread 2 prawns and 2 pieces of mango alternately on to each of 8 skewers. Place the skewers on an oiled barbecue grill over hot coals, brush them with the remaining marinade and cook for 2 minutes on each side, or until the prawns turn pink and are cooked through.

3 Serve 2 skewers on each plate, accompanied with some dressed salad.

1 tablespoon **sunflower oil**

4 tablespoons **lemon juice**

2 **garlic cloves**, crushed

1 teaspoon grated fresh **root ginger**

1 teaspoon **chilli powder**

1 tablespoon **honey**

1 teaspoon **sea salt**

16 large raw **tiger prawns**, peeled and deveined

1 large **mango**, peeled, pitted and cut into 16 bite-sized pieces

dressed **salad**, to serve

* plus 10 minutes marinating

5 tablespoons **olive oil**

2 tablespoons **balsamic vinegar**

2 tablespoons chopped **oregano** or **marjoram**

2 **garlic cloves**, crushed

pepper

12 large raw **king prawns**, peeled, but tails retained, and deveined then butterflied (see page 127)

PREP
20*

COOK
4

SERVES
4

stylish

Spiedini of prawns

A Mediterranean dish that is really mouthwatering. Cook plenty of prawns as they are always popular and will disappear in no time.

1 To make the marinade, mix together all the ingredients apart from the prawns in a large, shallow non-metallic dish. Add the prawns and turn to coat thoroughly. Cover and leave to marinate in the refrigerator for 1 hour.

2 Remove the prawns from the marinade and thread 3 prawns on to each of 4 skewers. Cook the prawns on an oiled barbecue grill over medium-hot coals for 3–4 minutes, turning them once and basting with any remaining marinade, until the flesh is opaque and just cooked. Serve immediately.

* plus 1 hour
  marinating

Prawn burgers with harissa

Harissa is a hot and piquant Moroccan sauce made from chillies, often served with seafood. A cucumber salad makes a good accompaniment to the burgers.

1 Place all the ingredients except for the polenta in a food processor. Process until the mixture comes together but still has a rough texture. Divide the mixture into 8 portions and shape each one into a ball, then flatten slightly into a burger. Cover and chill for 1 hour.

2 Spread the polenta on a large plate. Dip the burgers into the polenta and coat evenly, then cook them on an oiled barbecue grill over medium-hot coals for about 4 minutes on each side, turning them frequently, until they are cooked through. Meanwhile, whisk the dressing ingredients in a bowl, then set aside.

3 To assemble, wrap the pitta bread slices around the burgers, top each with a slice of lime and secure with a cocktail stick. Serve accompanied by the harissa dressing.

PREP
20*

COOK
8

SERVES
4

hot

150 g (5 oz) **white fish fillets**

425 g (14 oz) raw, peeled **tiger prawns**

75 g (3 oz) canned **water chestnuts**, drained and chopped

2.5 cm (1 inch) piece of fresh **root ginger**, peeled and grated

6 **spring onions**, finely chopped

1 teaspoon **harissa paste**

grated rind of 1 **lime**

125 g (4 oz) **polenta** or **cornmeal**

salt and **pepper**

HARISSA DRESSING

3 teaspoons **harissa paste**

3 tablespoons **olive oil**

juice of 1 **lime**

TO SERVE

4 **mini pitta breads**, sliced

1 **lime**, sliced

425 g (14 oz) fresh **white crab meat**

1 **egg**, beaten

2 tablespoons **Mayonnaise** (see page 236)

a good pinch of **English mustard powder**

2 tablespoons **lemon juice**

½ **red onion**, grated

3 tablespoons **chives**, chopped

few drops of **Tabasco sauce**

150 g (5 oz) **breadcrumbs**

salt and **pepper**

SWEETCORN SALSA

125 g (4 oz) frozen **sweetcorn kernels**

1 small **red onion**, finely chopped

1 **avocado**, finely chopped

2 tablespoons chopped **chives**

1 tablespoon **red wine vinegar**

2 tablespoons **olive oil**

salt and **pepper**

TO SERVE

4 **soft rolls**

salad leaves

moist

Crab cake burgers

These burgers can also be made with tinned crab meat; the result isn't quite the same, but they are still very tasty.

1 In a bowl, combine all the ingredients for the burgers, except for the breadcrumbs, and season lightly with salt and pepper. Divide the mixture into 4 portions and shape each one into a ball, then flatten slightly into a burger. Spread the breadcrumbs on a plate and coat each burger in them evenly. The mix is very wet so you may need to reshape the burgers in the crumbs. Cover and chill for 1 hour.

2 Meanwhile, make the salsa. Boil the sweetcorn for 2 minutes then drain and refresh under cold running water. Place the sweetcorn in a bowl with the remaining ingredients and mix thoroughly. Set aside until needed.

3 Cook the burgers on an oiled barbecue grill over medium-hot coals for 5–10 minutes on each side, or until heated through.

4 To assemble, halve and toast the rolls on the barbecue, fill with a little salad and a burger and serve with the salsa on the side.

* plus 1 hour chilling

Mussels and clams marinière

To make life easier serve the mussels and clams on a wooden board in their parcels. Eaten as a finger food they are even more delicious.

1 Place 2 large double pieces of heavy-duty foil on a work surface and bring the edges of the foil up slightly. Place the mussels on one piece and the clams on the other, adding 1 bay leaf and 1 sprig of thyme to each parcel.

2 Mix together all the remaining ingredients except the parsley and divide between the two parcels. Bring the edges of the parcels together and press to seal.

3 Cook the parcels on a barbecue grill over medium-hot coals for 5–10 minutes, shaking occasionally. When cooked, all the mussels and clams will be opened. (Discard any that have not). Tip the mussels and clams immediately into a large colander set over a bowl and strain the resulting juices through a muslin-lined sieve.

4 Serve the mussels and clams immediately with the strained cooking liquor poured over them and sprinkled with the chopped parsley.

PREP
30

COOK
10

SERVES
4

buttery

750 g (1½ lb) **mussels**, scrubbed well and debearded, any open ones discarded

750 g (1½ lb) **clams**, scrubbed well, any open ones discarded

2 **bay leaves**

2 sprigs of **thyme**

2 **shallots**, finely chopped

1 **garlic clove**, finely chopped

25 g (1 oz) **butter**, melted

½ teaspoon lightly crushed **peppercorns**

juice and finely grated rind of 2 **oranges**

200 ml (7 fl oz) **dry white wine**

2 tablespoons chopped **parsley**

vegetarian

125 g (4 oz) **red kidney beans**

125 g (4 oz) **brown rice**

1 tablespoon **groundnut oil**

1 **onion**, finely chopped

1 **garlic clove**, crushed

1 **green chilli**, deseeded and finely chopped

1 teaspoon **cumin seeds**

1 teaspoon **ground coriander**

½ teaspoon **ground turmeric**

2 **eggs**, beaten

a little light **olive oil**, for brushing

salt and **pepper**

NUTTY SAUCE

3 tablespoons chopped **coriander**

25 g (1 oz) **pistachio nuts**, chopped

2 **green chillies**, deseeded and finely chopped

125 ml (4 fl oz) **Greek yogurt**

salt and **pepper**

PREP
20*

COOK
80

SERVES
4

crumbly

Kidney bean and rice burgers

Make sure a crisp crust has formed on the underside of the patties before you try to turn them over and cook the other side. Add a final sprinkling of lime juice, if you like.

1 Put the beans in a bowl, cover with cold water and leave to soak overnight. Drain, rinse under cold running water and drain again. Put the beans in a saucepan, cover with fresh water and boil vigorously for 10 minutes. Lower the heat and simmer for 50–60 minutes, until tender. Drain, set aside to cool, then mash until smooth.

2 Meanwhile, put the rice into a pan of lightly salted boiling water, lower the heat and simmer for about 20–25 minutes until just cooked. Drain, refresh under cold running water, then drain well.

3 Heat the oil in a small frying pan and cook the onion, garlic and chilli for 5 minutes without browning the onion. Add the spices and cook for 1–2 minutes more, then add the contents of the frying pan to the mashed beans. Stir in the rice and mix well. Add the eggs, and salt and pepper to taste, then stir well to combine.

4 For the sauce, whizz the coriander, pistachios and chillies in a food processor until smooth. Transfer to a bowl, stir in the yogurt and season to taste.

5 Shape the bean and rice mixture into 4 burgers. Brush them with a little oil, then place on an oiled barbecue grill and cook over medium-hot coals for 8–10 minutes, turning once. Serve with the sauce.

* plus overnight soaking

Sweet potato, bean and feta burgers

Sun-dried tomato pesto can be found in jars in most supermarkets. If you are short of time it's not necessary to make your own.

1 First, make the pesto by blending together all the pesto ingredients in a food processor until you have a textured paste.

2 Boil the sweet potatoes in salted boiling water for 15 minutes or until soft. Drain and leave to cool then mash the sweet potatoes with the butter beans using a potato masher. Fold in the feta and sage and season to taste with salt and pepper, remembering that the feta is quite salty. Divide into 4 portions and form into balls, then flatten slightly into burgers.

3 Coat the burgers in the flour, then dip them first in the beaten egg and then in the breadcrumbs. Re-form into a burger shape if necessary and then cover and chill for 30 minutes.

4 Brush the burgers with a little oil and cook them on an oiled barbecue grill over medium-hot coals for 4–5 minutes on each side.

5 To assemble, halve and toast the buns or baps on the barbecue. Top each base with some salad, then a burger. Spoon over the pesto and pine nuts and serve immediately with extra pesto and the lid on the side.

PREP
25*

COOK
25

SERVES
4

cheesy

500 g (1 lb) **sweet potatoes**, cut into 2 cm (¾ inch) dice

300 g (10 oz) can **butter beans**, drained and rinsed

150 g (5 oz) **feta cheese**

2 tablespoons chopped **sage**

1 tablespoon **plain flour**

1 **egg**, beaten

75 g (3 oz) **dried breadcrumbs**

vegetable oil, for frying

salt and **pepper**

SUN-DRIED TOMATO PESTO

125 g (4 oz) **sun-dried tomatoes** in oil, drained

15 g (½ oz) **roasted pine nuts**

3 tablespoons chopped **basil leaves**

3 tablespoons **extra virgin olive oil**

TO SERVE

4 **burger buns** or **baps**

salad leaves

toasted pine nuts

* plus 30 minutes chilling

3 tablespoons **soy sauce**

1 tablespoon **rice wine vinegar**

1 teaspoon **sesame oil**

2.5 cm (1 inch) piece of fresh **root ginger**, peeled and grated

1 **garlic clove**, crushed

400 g (13 oz) firm **tofu**, cut into 4 square pieces

2 large **eggs**, beaten

75 g (3 oz) **breadcrumbs**

25 g (1 oz) **sesame seeds**

a little light **olive oil**, for brushing

ROASTED CHERRY TOMATOES

250 g (8 oz) **cherry tomatoes**

2 **garlic cloves**, chopped

2 tablespoons chopped **basil**

2 tablespoons **olive oil**

TO SERVE

4 **crusty rolls**

salad leaves

PREP
20*

COOK
25

SERVES
4

crispy

Crispy tofu burgers

If you add a sprinkle of sugar to the tomatoes before putting them in the oven they'll be even more tasty. They can also be cooked on the barbecue for ease.

1 To make the marinade, mix together the soy sauce, vinegar, sesame oil, ginger and garlic in a large, shallow non-metallic dish. Add the tofu and turn to cover well. Cover and leave to marinate for at least 1 hour, but preferably overnight.

2 To cook the roasted cherry tomatoes, put the tomatoes in a roasting tin and scatter with the garlic, basil and olive oil. Cook in a preheated oven, 200°C (400°F), Gas Mark 6, until the skins start to split, about 15 minutes. Set aside until needed (the tomatoes can be eaten hot or at room temperature).

3 To make the burgers, dip the tofu first into the beaten egg, then into the breadcrumbs and finally into the mixed sesame seeds. Dip each burger in the egg and then into the breadcrumbs again to make an extra thick coating.

4 Brush the burgers with a little oil and cook them on an oiled barbecue grill over medium-hot coals for 4–6 minutes on each side.

5 To assemble, halve and toast the rolls on the barbecue. Top each base with salad leaves and a crispy tofu burger. Spoon over the roasted cherry tomatoes and their juices and serve immediately with the lids on the side.

* plus 1 hour or overnight marinating

Portobello mushroom burgers

Portobello mushrooms are large, flat mushrooms. They have a dense, meaty texture and rustic flavour that are perfect for these burgers.

PREP
5

COOK
25

SERVES
4

zesty

1 Place the mushrooms in a baking tin and sprinkle them with the garlic and thyme. Drizzle over the olive oil and cook in a preheated oven, 200°C (400°F), Gas Mark 6, for 10 minutes.

2 Place a slice of red pepper and a slice of goats' cheese on each mushroom. Heat the butter in a nonstick frying pan and fry the breadcrumbs, lemon rind and parsley until the breadcrumbs just start to colour, about 3 minutes. Spoon the breadcrumb mixture over the mushrooms and season well with salt and pepper.

3 Cook the mushrooms on an oiled barbecue grill over medium-hot coals for 8–10 minutes until the cheese has started to melt.

4 To assemble, halve and toast the buns on the barbecue. Fill with rocket leaves and a mushroom. Garnish with extra rocket leaves and serve.

4 **portobello mushrooms**

2 **garlic cloves**, finely chopped

2 tablespoons chopped **thyme**

3 tablespoons **olive oil**

4 large slices of **roasted red pepper**

150 g (5 oz) **goats' cheese**, cut into 4 thick slices

25–50 g (1–2 oz) **butter**

125 g (4 oz) **breadcrumbs**

grated rind of 1 **lemon**

4 tablespoons finely chopped **parsley**

salt and **pepper**

TO SERVE

2 large **burger buns**

75 g (3 oz) **rocket leaves**, plus extra for garnish

5–6 tablespoons **vegetable oil**

1 **onion**, chopped

½ teaspoon crushed **chilli flakes**

2 **garlic cloves**, coarsely chopped

1 tablespoon **medium curry paste**

425 g (14 oz) can **cannellini beans**, rinsed and drained

175 g (6 oz) **ground almonds**

75 g (3 oz) chopped **honey-roasted almonds** or **salted almonds**

1 **egg**

200 ml (7 fl oz) **yogurt**

2 tablespoons chopped **mint**

1 tablespoon **lemon juice**

salt and **pepper**

sprigs of **mint**, to garnish

warm **Naan Bread** (see page 204), to serve

PREP
15

COOK
10

SERVES
4

nutty

Nut koftas with minted yogurt

Be sure to oil the barbecue rack well before you put the koftas on it. They are a little crumbly and may be difficult to turn if they stick.

1 Heat 3 tablespoons of the oil in a frying pan, add the onion and fry for 4 minutes. Add the chilli flakes, garlic and curry paste and fry for a further 1 minute.

2 Transfer the mixture to a food processor or blender with the beans, ground almonds, chopped almonds, egg and a little salt and pepper and whizz until the mixture starts to bind together.

3 With lightly floured hands, take about one-eighth of the mixture and mould it around a skewer, forming it into a sausage shape about 2.5 cm (1 inch) thick. Make 7 more koftas in the same way. Place them on an oiled barbecue grill over medium-hot coals and brush with a tablespoon of the oil. Cook the koftas for about 5 minutes, until golden, turning once.

4 Meanwhile, mix the yogurt and mint in a small serving bowl and season to taste with salt and pepper. In a separate bowl, mix the remaining oil, lemon juice and a little salt and pepper.

5 Brush the koftas with the lemon dressing and serve with the yogurt dressing, on warm naan bread garnished with mint sprigs.

Black bean kebabs with mango relish

Tinned black beans will work equally well in this recipe; and as an alternative to the mango in the relish you can try pineapple.

PREP
25*

COOK
80

SERVES
4

rich

125 g (4 oz) **dried black beans**

3 tablespoons **olive oil**

1 **onion**, very finely chopped

1 **garlic clove**, crushed

1 **red chilli**, deseeded and finely chopped

1 teaspoon **ground coriander**

1 tablespoon chopped **coriander**

2 **courgettes**

24 mixed red and yellow **cherry tomatoes**

boiled rice, to serve

MANGO RELISH

1 ripe **mango**, peeled and pitted

1 small **onion**, grated

1 **red chilli**, deseeded and finely chopped

1 cm (½ inch) piece of fresh **root ginger**, peeled and grated

salt and **pepper**

1 Put the beans in a bowl, cover with cold water and leave to soak overnight. Drain, rinse in a colander under cold running water and drain again. Put the beans in a saucepan, cover with fresh water and boil vigorously for 10 minutes. Lower the heat and simmer for about 40–50 minutes until tender. Drain well and set the beans aside.

2 To make the mango relish, place the flesh in a bowl and mash lightly. Add the onion, chilli and ginger and mix well. Season with a little salt and pepper and set aside.

3 Heat 2 tablespoons of the oil in a pan. Add the onion, garlic and chilli and cook for 5–10 minutes until the onion is softened. Add the ground coriander and cook for 1–2 minutes more. Turn the onion and spice mixture into a bowl, add the drained beans and coriander and mash well. Form the mixture into 24 balls.

4 Cut the courgettes lengthways into strips and brush with the remaining oil. Thread the bean balls on metal skewers alternating with the cherry tomatoes and weaving the courgette strips in between. Cook the kebabs on an oiled barbecue grill over medium-hot coals for 4 minutes on each side. Serve with the mango relish and rice.

* plus overnight soaking

2 teaspoons **Pesto** (see page 20)

1 **garlic clove**, crushed

4 tablespoons **lemon juice**

salt

6 tablespoons **olive oil**

2 thick slices of **Italian bread**, cut into chunks

8 **cherry tomatoes**

8 **sun-dried tomatoes in oil**, drained

200 g (7 oz) **feta cheese**, cubed

4 **black olives**, plus extra to serve

herby

Feta and cherry tomato kebabs

250 g (8 oz) mini mozzarella cheeses (bocconcini) or the same amount of haloumi cheese could be used instead of the feta.

1 To make the marinade, put the pesto in a bowl, stir in the garlic, lemon juice and salt, then whisk in the olive oil.

2 Toss the bread briefly in the marinade, then remove. Add the cherry tomatoes, sun-dried tomatoes and feta and leave for 30 minutes.

3 Thread the ingredients on to skewers, starting with a cube of bread and finishing with an olive. Cook on an oiled barbecue grill over hot coals for 2–3 minutes on each side, basting with the marinade until the bread is crisp and the cheese is just beginning to melt. Serve with extra olives.

* plus 30 minutes marinating

Stuffed mini peppers with tomato sauce

Miniature peppers stuffed with a creamy minted cheese are delicious as a starter. Do not be tempted to fill the peppers completely, or they may burst during cooking.

1 To make the tomato sauce, heat the oil in a saucepan, add the onion and the garlic and cook for 5 minutes, until softened but not coloured. Stir in the canned tomatoes and herbs and simmer gently for 10 minutes. Strain the sauce through a sieve set over a clean pan. Set aside.

2 Combine the goats' cheese, ricotta and mint in a bowl. Stir in the chilli, if using, and season to taste.

3 Make a small slit in the side of each mini pepper, then carefully scrape out the seeds and core with a teaspoon, keeping the pepper shells intact. Half-fill each pepper with stuffing.

4 Cook the filled peppers on an oiled barbecue grill over medium-hot coals for about 10–15 minutes, turning occasionally, until softened. Meanwhile, reheat the tomato sauce by placing the pan at the edge of the barbecue grill. Serve the peppers with the sauce and some Greek yogurt.

PREP
20

COOK
30

SERVES
4

creamy

125 g (4 oz) soft **goats' cheese**

50 g (2 oz) **ricotta**

1½ tablespoons chopped **mint**

1 **red** or **green chilli**, deseeded and finely chopped (optional)

8 **mini peppers**

salt and **pepper**

Greek yogurt, to serve

TOMATO SAUCE

1 tablespoon **olive oil**

1 **onion**, finely chopped

1 **garlic clove**, crushed

400 g (13 oz) can **tomatoes**

1 tablespoon chopped **parsley**

1 tablespoon chopped **oregano**

4–8 **vine leaves**, fresh or preserved in brine

1 tablespoon chopped **thyme leaves**

1 tablespoon chopped **flat leaf parsley**

1 tablespoon chopped **oregano**

1 teaspoon crushed **mixed peppercorns**

1 tablespoon **lemon juice**

4 small whole **goats' cheeses**

2 tablespoons **olive oil**

crusty bread and/or **salad leaves**, to serve

PREP
10

COOK
8

SERVES
4

fresh

Goats' cheese in vine leaves

Goats' cheese is delicious when wrapped and grilled in vine leaves. Choose small whole cheeses such as crottin de Chavignol.

1 If you are using vine leaves preserved in brine, rinse them well in a colander under cold running water. Bring a small saucepan of water to the boil, add the vine leaves and blanch for 1 minute. If using fresh vine leaves, remove any tough stems and blanch briefly in boiling water for 30 seconds. Regardless of type, refresh the blanched leaves under cold water, then drain well.

2 Mix the chopped fresh herbs with the crushed peppercorns and lemon juice in a shallow bowl. Brush the goats' cheeses with olive oil and roll them in the herb mixture. Wrap the coated cheeses in the vine leaves, then brush them with any remaining olive oil.

3 Cook the wrapped goats' cheeses on an oiled barbecue grill over medium-hot coals for 8 minutes, turning once, until the cheeses are just soft.

4 Serve the cheeses with toasted crusty bread and a few salad leaves as a starter, or serve on a bed of salad as part of a buffet meal.

Goats' cheese peppers with chilli relish

Try using 200 g (7 oz) of sliced mozzarella cheese instead of the goats' cheese for a different flavour.

PREP
10

COOK
25

SERVES
4

charred

1 To make the chilli relish, grill the chillies on an oiled barbecue grill over hot coals for 3–4 minutes until charred and tender. Put them into a plastic bag, seal and set aside until cool enough to handle. Remove the stalks and skin, cut the chillies in half and remove the seeds. Roughly chop the flesh, retaining the flavourful juices.

2 Place the chillies in a mortar and pound with a pestle. Stir in the remaining ingredients and season with salt. Set aside.

3 Cut the peppers in half lengthways and remove the seeds. Leave the stalks attached but trim away any white membrane. Place the peppers cut side down on an oiled barbecue grill over medium-hot coals and cook for 8–10 minutes until well charred. Turn the peppers over, place a slice of goats' cheese in the centre of each, sprinkle with the thyme and olive oil and leave to cook for a further 10 minutes or until the peppers have softened and the goats' cheese has melted.

4 Serve the peppers sprinkled with the chopped black olives and cracked black pepper, accompanied by the chilli relish.

2 **red peppers**

2 **yellow peppers**

2 small whole **goats' cheeses**, each cut into 4 slices

1 tablespoon **thyme leaves**

2 tablespoons **extra virgin olive oil**

25 g (1 oz) **pitted black olives**, finely chopped

cracked black **pepper**

CHILLI RELISH

6 large **red chillies**

2 tablespoons **lime juice**

2 **garlic cloves**, crushed

3 tablespoons chopped **flat leaf parsley** or **coriander**

sea salt

1½ tablespoons chopped **oregano**

2 tablespoons **extra virgin olive oil**

1 **garlic clove**, crushed

2 tablespoons **lemon juice**

250 g (8 oz) **haloumi cheese**, cut into 4 pieces or lots of small cubes

1 large head of **radicchio**

PREP
10

COOK
8

SERVES
4

rustic

Haloumi wrapped in radicchio

These parcels make a tasty starter served with crusty bread, or they can be eaten as a main course with new potatoes.

1 Mix together the oregano, olive oil, garlic and lemon juice in a bowl, add the haloumi pieces and toss to coat.

2 Remove the stalk and core from the radicchio and gently pull the leaves apart. Lay 3–4 leaves on a work surface and place a quarter of the haloumi mixture in the centre. Wrap the radicchio around the cheese, and then over-wrap in a piece of double-thickness foil. Repeat with the remaining radicchio and cheese mixture.

3 Cook the parcels on an oiled barbecue grill over medium coals for 3–4 minutes on each side. Remove from the heat and serve immediately.

Radicchio with pears and Roquefort

The slight bitterness of the radicchio combines well with the citrus-sweetness of the baked pears and the creamy sharp blue Roquefort.

1 Cut each pear into quarters lengthways and remove the cores. Place the pears in a single layer on a large sheet of double-thickness foil, turning up the edges slightly. Mix the orange rind and juice and honey in a jug and pour over the pears.

2 Bring up the edges of the foil and press together to seal. Cook the parcel on a barbecue grill over medium-hot coals for about 15–20 minutes or until the pears are tender.

3 About 6 minutes before the pears are ready, cook the radicchio. Cut each head into quarters, brush with the walnut oil and cook on the grill for 2–3 minutes on each side.

4 To serve, divide the pears and their cooking juices between 4 plates. Add 4 radicchio quarters to each portion, then sprinkle with the crumbled Roquefort and a little pepper.

PREP
5

COOK
20

SERVES
4

zesty

4 ripe **pears**, such as Conference

finely grated rind and juice of 2 **oranges**

4 tablespoons clear **honey**

4 small heads of **radicchio**

1 tablespoon **walnut oil**

125 g (4 oz) **Roquefort cheese**, crumbled

pepper

25 g (1 oz) **butter**

250 g (8 oz) **young leaf spinach**

grated **nutmeg**

8 **baby brioche rolls**

8 **quails' eggs**

salt and **pepper**

HOLLANDAISE SAUCE

175 g (6 oz) **butter**

3 **egg yolks**

2 tablespoons **water**

1 tablespoon **lemon juice**

salt and **pepper**

PREP
15

COOK
45

SERVES
4

classic

Baby brioches Florentine

These make a great addition to a breakfast or brunch barbecue. If you are short of time, buy ready-made hollandaise sauce, though it won't be quite as delicious as your own.

1 Melt the butter in a large saucepan. Wash the spinach and add it to the pan with only the water that clings to the leaves. Cover the pan and cook for about 3–4 minutes, stirring once, until the spinach has just wilted. Drain well and transfer to a bowl. Add salt and plenty of nutmeg and pepper to taste.

2 Cut a neat slice off the top of each brioche roll and set aside, then remove sufficient crumbs from each roll to form a hollow. Place a spoonful of spinach in each hollow and carefully crack a quail's egg over the top. Replace the brioche lids. Wrap each roll in a double thickness of foil and place right side up on a barbecue grill. Cook over medium-hot coals for 30–40 minutes until the eggs are just set.

3 To make the hollandaise sauce, first melt the butter in a small pan over a low heat, then remove from the heat and leave to cool slightly. Mix the egg yolks and water in a large heatproof bowl. Set this over a large saucepan of barely simmering water and whisk until light, creamy and pale in colour.

4 Using a ladle, gradually add the melted butter in a thin stream, whisking constantly and avoiding the white milky residue at the bottom of the pan. Carry on whisking until the mixture is a thick, foamy sauce. Remove from the heat and season with lemon juice, salt and pepper. Serve with the brioche.

Mediterranean kebabs

PREP
20*

COOK
8

SERVES
4

fun

These tasty kebabs can easily be adapted with a quick change of vegetables. Try using thick slices of fennel, cubes of aubergine and shiitake or button mushrooms instead.

1 Trim the courgettes, then use a vegetable peeler to cut them lengthways into very thin slices or ribbons. Place the courgettes in a shallow bowl and add the tomatoes, onion and red pepper.

2 Mix the oil, parsley, lemon juice and garlic and season with salt and pepper, then pour this mixture over the vegetables and set them aside to marinate for at least 5 minutes.

3 Thread the vegetables on to 8 medium or 4 large metal skewers, making sure there is a variety of vegetables on each skewer and threading the strips of courgette between and around the other vegetables. Alternatively, you can roll up the courgette strips and thread the rolls on to the skewers. Reserve the juices from the marinade.

4 Brush the vegetables with the reserved marinade, then cook them on an oiled barbecue grill over medium-hot coals for about 6–8 minutes, turning frequently, until the vegetables are tender. Serve sprinkled with thyme.

2 **courgettes**

12 **cherry tomatoes**

1 **red onion**, cut into 8 wedges

1 **red pepper**, cored, deseeded and cut into 2.5 cm (1 inch) squares

2 tablespoons **olive oil**

1 tablespoon finely chopped **flat leaf parsley**

4 tablespoons **lemon juice**

1 **garlic clove**, crushed

salt and **pepper**

chopped **thyme**, to garnish

* plus 5 minutes marinating

2 **fennel bulbs**

1 **lemon**

LEMON AND
OLIVE DRESSING

2 tablespoons **lemon juice**

1 **garlic clove**, crushed

8 tablespoons **extra virgin olive oil**

75 g (3 oz) **pitted black olives**, finely chopped

sea salt and **pepper**

PREP
15

COOK
8

SERVES
4

zesty

Fennel, lemon and black olive kebabs

Your vegetarian friends will love these crunchy, zesty kebabs. Serve with Turkish flatbreads to mop up the juices and a tomato and basil salad.

1 To make the lemon and olive dressing, whisk together the lemon juice, garlic and 6 tablespoons of the olive oil in a bowl. Stir in the chopped black olives and season with sea salt and pepper.

2 Cut the fennel bulbs lengthways into 8 wedges, making sure each wedge is attached to a little of the core. Cut the lemon into 8 wedges.

3 Thread the fennel and lemon wedges alternately on to 4 skewers and brush them all over with the remaining olive oil. Place the kebabs on an oiled barbecue grill and cook over medium-hot coals for about 4 minutes on each side. Serve the kebabs drizzled with the lemon and olive dressing.

Baby aubergines with yogurt

For ease of cooking and turning, the baby aubergines can be threaded on skewers if you like.

1 To make the herbed Greek yogurt, mix all the ingredients and set aside. Make it well ahead so the flavours have time to mingle.

2 Slice all the baby aubergines in half lengthways, leaving them attached to their stalks. Using a small brush, coat the aubergines with olive oil. Cook on an oiled barbecue grill over medium-hot coals for about 2–3 minutes on each side.

3 To serve, place the aubergines on a serving dish or plate and spoon over the herbed yogurt. Serve with toasted pitta breads, if liked.

PREP
20

COOK
6

SERVES
8

herby

24 **baby aubergines**

6 tablespoons **olive oil**

toasted **pitta breads**, to serve (optional)

HERBED GREEK YOGURT

4 tablespoons chopped **parsley**

4 tablespoons chopped **dill**

4 tablespoons chopped **mint**

1 **red onion**, finely chopped

4 **garlic cloves**, crushed

150 g (5 oz) **Kalamata olives**, pitted and sliced

4 tablespoons **fennel seeds**, crushed

2 tablespoons **capers**, chopped

25 g (1 oz) **gherkins**, finely chopped

finely grated rind and juice of 2 **limes**

300 ml (½ pint) strained **Greek yogurt**

salt and **pepper**

1 tablespoon **groundnut oil**

1 tablespoon dark **soy sauce**, plus extra to serve

1 tablespoon **balsamic vinegar**

1 tablespoon **wholegrain barley miso**

1 teaspoon **stem ginger syrup** (from a jar)

2 **aubergines**, cut lengthways into 5 mm (¼ inch) thick slices

green salad sprinkled with **sesame seeds**, to serve

PREP
5*

COOK
8

SERVES
2–4

delicate

Aubergine steaks with miso

Try using 5 courgettes in place of the aubergines, cutting them into slices of the same thickness.

1 Combine the oil, soy sauce, vinegar, miso and ginger syrup and brush all over the aubergines. Set aside to marinate for 15 minutes.

2 Cook the aubergines on an oiled barbecue grill over medium coals for 2–4 minutes on each side until charred and tender, basting frequently with the marinade. Serve the aubergines with a little extra soy sauce for dipping and accompanied by a green salad sprinkled with sesame seeds.

* plus 15 minutes
marinating

Vegetables with olive and walnut paste

Choose a selection of vegetables in season to serve with this rich green olive and walnut paste. Asparagus and fennel are excellent when barbecued.

1 To make the olive and walnut paste, place the olives, fresh and pickled walnuts, garlic and parsley in a food processor or blender and whizz until finely chopped. With the motor running, gradually add the olive oil in a thin, steady stream until the mixture forms a stiff paste. Scrape into a bowl and season with salt and pepper.

2 Brush the aubergines, peppers, courgettes and leeks with the olive oil. Place on an oiled barbecue grill over medium-hot coals and cook the aubergine and peppers for 6–8 minutes and the courgettes and leeks for 3 minutes until tender, turning frequently.

3 Brush the bread with any remaining olive oil and toast on the barbecue until golden. Spread the toast with the olive and walnut paste and top with the hot vegetables.

PREP
6

COOK
10

SERVES
4

nutty

1 large **aubergine**, cut into slices 1 cm (½ inch) thick

2 **red peppers** and 2 **yellow peppers**, halved, cored and deseeded but stalks left on

2 **courgettes**, cut lengthways into 5 mm (¼ inch) slices

8 **baby leeks**, rinsed well

6 tablespoons **olive oil**

4 large slices of **crusty bread**

OLIVE AND WALNUT PASTE

75 g (3 oz) **pitted green olives**

75 g (3 oz) **walnut pieces**

25 g (1 oz) bottled **pickled walnuts**, drained

2 **garlic cloves**, crushed

25 g (1 oz) **parsley**

125 ml (4 fl oz) **extra virgin olive oil**

salt and **pepper**

2 tablespoons **balsamic vinegar**

1–2 **garlic cloves**, crushed

375 g (12 oz) **tomatoes**, skinned (see page 13), deseeded and chopped

7 tablespoons **olive oil**

500 g (1 lb) **young asparagus spears**, woody stems removed

50 g (2 oz) **pine nuts**, toasted

25 g (1 oz) **Parmesan cheese**, shaved into thin slivers

sea salt flakes and **pepper**

PREP
15

COOK
6

SERVES
4

fresh

Asparagus with balsamic tomato coulis

Asparagus is perfect for the barbecue as it cooks quickly and easily.

1   Place the vinegar, garlic, chopped tomatoes and 5 tablespoons of the olive oil in a small bowl. Mix well to combine and set aside.

2   Brush the asparagus spears with the remaining olive oil and cook on an oiled barbecue grill over medium-hot coals for about 5–6 minutes, or until the spears are tender.

3   Divide the grilled asparagus between 4 warmed plates. Spoon over the balsamic vinegar and tomato dressing, top with the pine nuts and Parmesan slivers and sprinkle with the sea salt flakes and pepper. Serve at once.

Sweetcorn with skorthalia

Skorthalia is a garlic sauce that can also be served with other vegetables, or grilled meat or fish. It goes particularly well with barbecued courgette and fennel wedges.

1 To make the skorthalia, place the breadcrumbs in a bowl and cover with water. Soak for 5 minutes, then squeeze out the excess liquid and place the crumbs in a food processor or blender. Add the ground almonds, garlic and 1 tablespoon of the lemon juice and whizz until mixed. With the motor running, gradually add the olive oil in a thin, steady stream until the mixture resembles mayonnaise. Add more lemon juice and salt and pepper to taste.

2 Pull down the outer leaves of the sweetcorn cobs and remove the inner skins. Pull the leaves back over the corn cobs. Cook on a barbecue grill over hot coals for about 30–40 minutes, until the kernels are juicy and come away from the core easily.

3 To serve, pull back the leaves of the corn cobs and spread with the skorthalia.

PREP **15**

COOK **40**

SERVES **4**

crunchy

4 whole **corn cobs**, with husks

SKORTHALIA

50 g (2 oz) **white breadcrumbs**

75 g (3 oz) **ground almonds**

4 **garlic cloves**, crushed

2 tablespoons **lemon juice**

150 ml (¼ pint) **extra virgin olive oil**

salt and **pepper**

75 g (3 oz) **walnut halves**

175 g (6 oz) **crème fraîche**

1½ tablespoons **wholegrain mustard**

3 tablespoons snipped **chives**, plus extra to garnish

8 **raw beetroot**

salt and **pepper**

Beetroot with mustard and walnut sauce

This recipe is very economical of barbecue space as the beetroot are cooked in the coals, leaving the grill rack free for other food.

1 Roast the walnuts on a baking sheet in a preheated oven, 180°C (350°F), Gas Mark 4, for about 8–10 minutes until they are golden. Leave to cool, then chop roughly. Reserve 3 tablespoons of the nuts for garnish, and put the rest in a bowl.

2 Stir in the crème fraîche, mustard and snipped chives. Season with salt and pepper to taste.

3 Meanwhile, wrap each beetroot in a double thickness of foil. Place in the embers of the hot barbecue and cook for about 40–50 minutes, or until tender.

4 Unwrap the foil, split open the beetroot and top with the sauce, sprinkle with the reserved walnuts and garnish with extra chives.

Red chilli polenta chips

PREP
10

COOK
35

Polenta is the Italian name for the bright yellow cornmeal that is known in the United States as cornmeal mush.

1 Bring the measurement water and salt to the boil in a large pan. Pour in the polenta in a thin, steady stream, stirring all the time. Continue to stir the mixture, beating it as it thickens, for about 20 minutes until it leaves the sides of the pan.

2 Immediately stir in the Parmesan, sun-dried tomatoes and chopped red chillies. Tip the polenta out on to a board or baking sheet. Leave to cool, then cut into chunky chips.

3 Bring a small pan of water to the boil and add the garlic cloves. Reduce the heat and simmer them for 10 minutes, then drain. When they are cool enough to handle, skewer 3 garlic cloves on to each of 4 presoaked cocktail sticks.

4 Brush the polenta chips and garlic skewers with the oil and cook on an oiled barbecue grill over medium-hot coals for about 3 minutes on each side, until the garlic is soft and the polenta chips are charred and golden.

SERVES
4

garlicky

750 ml (1¼ pints) **water**

1 teaspoon **salt**

250 g (8 oz) **polenta**

50 g (2 oz) finely grated **Parmesan cheese**

8 **sun-dried tomatoes** in oil, drained and finely chopped

4 large **red chillies**, grilled, peeled, deseeded and finely chopped (see page 147)

12 **garlic cloves**, unpeeled

6 tablespoons **olive oil**

salads

1 small **French baguette**

2 **garlic cloves**, crushed

2 tablespoons **olive oil**

125 g (4 oz) **baby spinach leaves**

1 ripe **pear**, cut into fine wedges

BLUE CHEESE DRESSING

1 tablespoon **lemon juice**

50 g (2 oz) **soft blue cheese**, such as Roquefort

1 tablespoon **Mayonnaise** (see page 236)

3 tablespoons **crème fraîche** or **soured cream**

PREP
15

COOK
10

SERVES
4

rustic

Spinach, pear and garlic toast salad

The strong flavours of the blue cheese and garlic are offset in this pretty salad by the milder spinach and pear. The combination of soft pear and crisp toast is a winner.

1 Slice the baguette at an angle into slices that are so thin you can just see through the bread.

2 Mix the garlic and oil and brush over the bread. Place on a baking sheet and bake in a preheated oven, 200°C (400°F), Gas Mark 6, for 10 minutes or until crisp and golden. Remove and leave to cool.

3 To serve, arrange the spinach, pear and crisp garlic toasts on a large serving platter. Whisk together the dressing ingredients in a small bowl and drizzle over the salad.

Celery and fennel salad

PREP
20

SERVES
4–6

light

Fennel, with its light aniseed flavour, is delicious combined with celery, pears and pecan nuts in this refreshing salad.

1 To make the blue cheese dressing, put the ingredients in a food processor or blender and process until smooth. Alternatively, mix in a bowl and mash with a fork. Stir in the spring onions and 50 g (2 oz) of the pecans.

2 Put the pear cubes in a bowl and mix with the lemon juice, then add the sliced fennel and celery.

3 To serve, arrange the salad leaves on individual serving plates or bowls. Top with the fennel, celery and pear mixture, spoon over the blue cheese dressing, season with pepper and sprinkle with the remaining pecans.

3 **spring onions**, finely sliced

75 g (3 oz) **pecans**, finely chopped

2 **pears**, peeled, halved, cored and cut into cubes

½ tablespoon **lemon juice**

1 **fennel bulb**, trimmed and finely sliced

4 **celery sticks**, finely sliced

pepper

escarole lettuce and **watercress**, to serve

BLUE CHEESE DRESSING

75 g (3 oz) **Roquefort** or **Gorgonzola cheese**

50 g (2 oz) **crème fraîche** or **soured cream**

1 tablespoon **red wine vinegar**

½ **cucumber**, peeled if preferred

1 small **round lettuce**, torn

1 small **Cos lettuce**, shredded

3 firm but ripe **tomatoes**, cut into wedges

1 **Spanish onion**, thinly sliced into rings

1 **green pepper**, cored, deseeded and thinly sliced into rings

125 g (4 oz) **feta cheese**, crumbled

12 or more **Kalamata olives**

1–2 tablespoons coarsely chopped **parsley**

2 teaspoons chopped **oregano**

salt

VINAIGRETTE

4 tablespoons **olive oil**

1 tablespoon **red wine vinegar**

1 **garlic clove**, crushed

salt and **pepper**

PREP
30*

SERVES
4

classic

Greek country salad

This traditional salad immediately evokes the atmosphere of Greece. It is found in Greek tavernas all over the world.

1 Whisk together the dressing ingredients in a small bowl. Cover and set aside for 1 hour.

2 Halve the cucumber lengthways, scoop out the seeds and cut into thin slices. Sprinkle with salt and leave to drain for 30 minutes. Rinse the cucumber and dry with kitchen paper.

3 Whisk the oil and vinegar again, then toss a little of it with the lettuce in a bowl. Layer the tomatoes, cucumber, onion, green pepper, cheese and olives on top of the lettuce.

4 Pour over the remaining dressing, then scatter over the chopped parsley and oregano and serve.

* plus 1 hour
standing and
30 minutes salting

Pasta, broad bean and pecorino salad

Orecchiette go very well with this mixture of sharp pecorino cheese and sweet baby broad beans. Serve with a selection of barbecued vegetables.

1 Blanch the broad beans a saucepan of lightly salted water for 1 minute. Drain, refresh under cold water, then drain again. Pop the beans out of their skins with your fingers.

2 Bring a large saucepan of boiling water to the boil with a little oil and salt, drop in the pasta and cook for 12–15 minutes, or until just tender. Drain the pasta in a colander, refresh under cold water and drain thoroughly.

3 Tip the pasta into a large salad bowl and add the remaining ingredients. Toss well, add plenty of pepper and serve.

PREP
10

COOK
15

SERVES
4

rustic

750 g (1½ lb) **fresh young broad beans** in the pod, shelled, or 250 g (8 oz) **frozen broad beans**, thawed

5 tablespoons **extra virgin olive oil**

500 g (1 lb) **orecchiette** or similar short pasta shapes

75 g (3 oz) **Pecorino cheese**, grated

50 g (2 oz) **pitted black olives**, finely chopped

5 tablespoons chopped **flat leaf parsley**

1 tablespoon **balsamic vinegar**

salt and **pepper**

1 **aubergine**

1 **red pepper**, halved, cored and deseeded

1 **yellow pepper**, halved, cored and deseeded

1 **courgette**

4 **garlic cloves**

4 tablespoons **extra virgin olive oil**

1 teaspoon **coarse sea salt**

300 g (10 oz) cooked **flageolet beans**

2 tablespoons chopped **mixed herbs** (such as parsley and oregano or coriander and mint)

6 tablespoons **Vinaigrette** (see page 164)

pepper

mint leaves, to garnish

PREP
15

COOK
40

SERVES
4

tasty

Flageolet bean and roasted vegetable salad

To ring the changes, try other vegetables in this salad, such as fennel, tomatoes, baby squash and mild chillies.

1 Cut all the vegetables into strips and place in a roasting tin. Add the garlic cloves. Sprinkle over the olive oil, sea salt and pepper.

2 Place in a preheated oven at 200°C (400°F), Gas Mark 6, and roast for 40 minutes. Transfer to a shallow bowl and leave to cool.

3 Add the beans to the roasted vegetables and toss lightly. Stir the herbs into the vinaigrette, then pour it over the salad and serve garnished with mint.

Puy lentil and red pepper salad

To save time buy tinned Puy lentils – they can be found in most good supermarkets and work just as well as the dried ones.

1 Place the lentils in a large saucepan with the measurement water, the studded onion and the bay leaves. Bring to a boil and boil for 10 minutes, then reduce the heat, cover and simmer gently for 15 minutes until the lentils are just tender. Drain well and remove the onion and bay leaves.

2 Meanwhile, grill the pepper quarters, skin side down, on an oiled barbecue grill over hot coals for 6–8 minutes until charred and tender. Put them into a plastic bag, seal and set aside until they are cool enough to handle. Peel off the skin and slice the flesh into strips.

3 Mix together the coriander seeds, olive oil, lemon juice and garlic in a serving bowl, add the drained lentils and red pepper strips. Toss together well, season to taste and serve.

PREP
10

COOK
25

SERVES
6–8

fresh

375 g (12 oz) **dried Puy lentils**

1.2 litres (2 pints) cold **water**

1 small **onion**, studded with 2 cloves

2 **bay leaves**

3 **red peppers**, deseeded and cut into quarters

1½ teaspoons **coriander seeds**, crushed

5 tablespoons **olive oil**

2–3 tablespoons **lemon juice**

2 **garlic cloves**, crushed

salt and **pepper**

175 g (6 oz) **dried chickpeas**

3 **red peppers**, deseeded and cut into quarters

12 **black olives**, pitted

2 tablespoons chopped **coriander**

ORANGE DRESSING

3 tablespoons **sunflower oil**

¼ teaspoon grated **orange rind**

2 tablespoons **orange juice**

1 **garlic clove**, crushed

salt and **pepper**

PREP
10

COOK
120

SERVES
4

zesty

Red pepper and chickpea salad

For a speedy alternative, try using cooked, canned chickpeas. Neither you or your guests will be able to tell the difference!

1 Put the beans in a bowl, cover with cold water and leave to soak overnight. Drain, rinse in a colander under cold running water and drain again. Cook the chickpeas in unsalted boiling water for 2 hours or until they are tender.

2 Meanwhile, grill the pepper quarters, skin side down, on an oiled barbecue grill over hot coals for 6–8 minutes until charred and tender. Put them into a plastic bag, seal and set aside until they are cool enough to handle. Peel off the skin and slice the flesh into strips.

3 Whisk together all the dressing ingredients in a bowl. Drain the chickpeas and toss in the orange dressing while they are still hot. Set aside to cool.

4 Stir in the red peppers, olives and coriander. Turn the salad into a serving dish and serve.

Asian salad

PREP
15*

SERVES
4

crunchy

The fish sauce in this dressing gives the salad an authentic Asian flavour. You can use nam pla, nuoc mam or nuoc nam, which you can find in most supermarkets or Asian stores.

1 Place the shredded spring onions and bean sprouts in iced water and leave for 30 minutes, then remove and drain well.

2 In a large serving bowl, toss the onion and sprouts with the lettuce leaves, cucumber, mint, basil and coriander.

3 Whisk together all the dressing ingredients in a small bowl or jug and pour over the salad. Serve immediately.

1 bunch of **spring onions**, shredded

50 g (2 oz) **bean sprouts**

3 **Baby Gem lettuces**, leaves separated

1 **cucumber**, cut into ribbons with a vegetable peeler

1 small bunch of **mint**, torn

1 small bunch of **basil**, torn

1 small bunch of **coriander**, torn

ASIAN DRESSING

2 tablespoons light **olive oil**

grated rind and juice of 1 **lime**

1 large **red chilli**, deseeded and finely chopped

1 tablespoon **Asian fish sauce**

1 tablespoon light **soy sauce**

pinch of **caster sugar**

250 g (8 oz) **bulgar wheat**

1 **fennel bulb**, very finely sliced

1 **red onion**, finely sliced

5 tablespoons chopped **mint**

5 tablespoons chopped **parsley**

2 tablespoons **fennel seeds**, crushed

2 tablespoons **olive oil**

finely grated rind and juice of 2 **lemons**

salt and **pepper**

PREP
15*

SERVES
6

tasty

Tabbouleh and fennel salad

Fennel adds its crunch to this moist bulgar wheat salad. Its aniseedy flavour is echoed in fennel seeds in the dressing.

1 Place the bulgar wheat in a bowl, add enough cold water to cover, then set aside for 30 minutes, until all the water has been absorbed. Line a colander with muslin or a clean tea towel. Drain the bulgar wheat into the colander, then gather up the sides of the cloth or tea towel and squeeze to extract as much of the liquid as possible from the bulgar wheat. Tip the wheat into a salad bowl.

2 Stir in the fennel, onion, mint, parsley, fennel seeds, oil, lemon rind and half the lemon juice. Season with salt and pepper to taste. Cover the bowl and set aside for 30 minutes to allow the flavours to develop, then taste the salad and add more lemon juice if required.

* plus 30 minutes
soaking and
30 minutes standing

Fennel and orange salad

PREP
15

SERVES
4

citrussy

Using an aged vinegar will give more depth of flavour without adding overpowering acidity. It's a product well worth having in your storecupboard.

1 Whisk together the dressing ingredients in a small bowl and set aside until needed.

2 Separate the chicory and radicchio into leaves and arrange on a large platter. Layer the fennel and orange slices over the salad leaves.

3 Drizzle the dressing over the salad, scatter with the pomegranate seeds and serve.

1 large head **chicory**

1 large head **radicchio**

2 small **fennel bulbs**, finely sliced

3 **oranges**, segmented

seeds from ½ **pomegranate**

RED WINE AND HONEY DRESSING

3 tablespoons **olive oil**

1 tablespoon aged **red wine vinegar**

1 tablespoon clear **honey**

salt and **pepper**

2 teaspoons **cumin seeds**

4 large **oranges**

125 g (4 oz) **green olives**, pitted and halved

50 ml (2 fl oz) **olive oil**

1 tablespoon **harissa paste** (optional)

1 crisp **lettuce**, torn into bite-sized pieces

salt

sprigs of **dill**, to garnish

PREP
15

COOK
5

SERVES
4

spicy

Orange and olive salad

The oranges that work best for this salad have a sharp flavour, not a sweet taste. The olives should be large and fleshy.

1 Heat a small heavy-based frying pan, add the cumin seeds and dry-fry until fragrant. Tip into a spice grinder and grind to a powder.

2 Remove the rind from 1 of the oranges with a zester and set aside. Peel the oranges with a sharp knife, carefully removing all the pith. Working over a bowl to catch the juice, cut out the segments from the oranges and discard any pips. Put the oranges and olives into a bowl with the juice.

3 Whisk or shake together the oil, harissa, if using, and roasted cumin. Add salt to taste, then pour the dressing over the oranges and olives and toss together.

4 Arrange the lettuce leaves in a serving dish and add the orange and olive mixture. Garnish with the reserved orange rind and sprigs of dill and serve.

Red cabbage coleslaw with almonds

PREP
20*

SERVES
4

tasty

This interesting take on the classic coleslaw has far more colour and certainly far more taste than the everyday variety.

1 In a large bowl, mix together the cabbage, onion, carrot, orange pepper and almonds.

2 Whisk together the dressing ingredients in a small bowl and pour over the shredded vegetables. Leave to stand for 30 minutes before serving.

¼ **red cabbage**, cored and shredded

1 small **red onion**, finely sliced

1 **carrot**, grated

1 **orange pepper**, cored, deseeded and shredded

50 g (2 oz) sliced **almonds**, dry-roasted

WHOLEGRAIN
MUSTARD DRESSING

juice of 1 **orange**

1 tablespoon **wholegrain mustard**

1 **garlic clove**, crushed

3 tablespoons **olive oil**

salt and **pepper**

* plus 30 minutes
standing

1 unpeeled **dessert apple**, cored and diced

2 **carrots**, grated

2 tablespoons diced **gherkins**

2 teaspoons **capers**

2 tablespoons chopped **parsley**

¼–½ **white cabbage** or **cabbage heart**, shredded

SPICED DRESSING

3 tablespoons **Mayonnaise** (see page 236)

½ teaspoon **curry powder**

½ teaspoon **ground nutmeg**

½ teaspoon **paprika**

1 teaspoon **English mustard**

1 tablespoon **olive oil**

1 tablespoon **lemon juice**

salt and **pepper**

PREP
15

SERVES
4

crisp

Spiced coleslaw

Avoid making the coleslaw too far ahead, as the cabbage and other ingredients should remain as fresh and crisp as possible.

1 Whisk together the dressing ingredients in a large bowl.

2 Add the apple, carrots, gherkins, capers and parsley to the dressing. Mix together thoroughly, then add the cabbage and mix again.

Rocket, red pepper and beetroot salad

This colourful dish is a real taste explosion. You could also serve it as a main course with some soft boiled eggs.

1 Cook the beetroot in salted boiling water for 45 minutes or until just done, then drain. Peel off the skin under cold running water. Cut each beetroot into 6–8 segments and arrange in a roasting dish. Drizzle with the oil and roast in a preheated oven, 200°C (400°F), Gas Mark 6, for 30 minutes or until cooked through and slightly charred around the edges.

2 To make the dressing, put half the hazelnuts, the vinegar, garlic and oil into a food processor and process until smooth. Season generously with salt and pepper.

3 Place the rocket leaves, red pepper and roasted beetroot on a large plate and scatter over the remaining hazelnuts. Drizzle the dressing over the salad and serve immediately.

PREP
10

COOK
75

SERVES
4

peppery

4 raw **beetroot**

1 tablespoon **olive oil**

75 g (3 oz) **rocket leaves**

300 g (10 oz) jar **chargrilled red peppers**, drained

ROASTED HAZELNUT AND BALSAMIC DRESSING

50 g (2 oz) **roasted hazelnuts**, roughly chopped

1 tablespoon **balsamic vinegar**

1 **garlic clove**, crushed

4 tablespoons light **olive oil** or **hazelnut oil**

salt and **pepper**

2 **cucumbers**

6 tablespoons **sea salt**

1 bunch of **radishes**, trimmed and thinly sliced

MUSTARD DRESSING

1 **egg yolk**

1 tablespoon **coarse-grain mustard**

1 tablespoon clear **honey**

2 tablespoons **lemon juice**

3 tablespoons **olive oil**

3 tablespoons chopped **dill**

pepper

PREP
15*

SERVES
4–6

hot

Cucumber, radish and dill salad

To ring the changes on this salad, omit the honey and replace the dill with 3 tablespoons of parsley, tarragon or basil.

1 Cut both the cucumbers in half lengthways, scoop out the seeds and slice very thinly.

2 Layer the cucumber slices in a colander and sprinkle with the salt. Set the colander over a plate or in the sink to catch the juices and leave for 1–1½ hours. Rinse well under cold water, drain and pat the slices dry with a clean tea towel. Place in a salad bowl and add the radishes.

3 To make the dressing, whisk together the egg yolk, mustard, honey, pepper and lemon juice in a small bowl. Continue to whisk while gradually adding the oil in a thin, steady stream until well amalgamated, then stir in the chopped dill. Add the dressing to the cucumber and radishes, toss well and serve.

* plus 1–1½ hours
salting

Watercress and pomegranate salad

This colourful and unusual salad is a stunning accompaniment to barbecued meat and game.

PREP
15

SERVES
4

fragrant

1 Break open the pomegranate and scoop out the seeds, discarding the bitter yellow pith. Place the seeds in a large bowl with the watercress.

2 Finely grate the rind from 2 of the oranges, then set aside. Working carefully over the bowl with the pomegranate and watercress so that no juice is wasted, peel and segment all the oranges and carefully remove the membrane around each segment. Add the orange segments to the bowl.

3 In a separate bowl, combine the remaining ingredients and the reserved grated orange rind. Mix well, pour over the salad, season with a few sea salt flakes and serve.

1 **pomegranate**

1 bunch of **watercress**, broken into sprigs

4 **oranges**

1 teaspoon **rosewater** or **orange flower water**

5 tablespoons **olive oil**

1 tablespoon **raspberry vinegar** or **white wine vinegar**

½ teaspoon **pink peppercorns** in brine, drained

sea salt flakes

250 g (8 oz) mixed red and yellow **baby tomatoes** (plum tomatoes, if possible), cut in half

250 g (8 oz) thin **green beans**, trimmed

handful of **mint**, chopped

1 **garlic clove**, crushed

4 tablespoons **extra virgin olive oil**

1 tablespoon **balsamic vinegar**

salt and **pepper**

PREP
10

COOK
2

SERVES
4

classic

Tomato and green bean salad

This dish is also delicious if you roast the tomatoes lightly before adding them to the salad. Leave them whole and thread on to skewers. Cook for 1–2 minutes on each side over medium-hot coals.

1 Put the baby tomatoes in a large bowl.

2 Blanch the green beans in a saucepan of lightly salted boiling water for 2 minutes, then drain well and place in the bowl with the tomatoes.

3 Add the remaining ingredients, season with salt and pepper and mix well. Serve warm or cold.

Carrot and celeriac salad

PREP
15

SERVES
4–6

zesty

250 g (8 oz) **carrots**

250 g (8 oz) **celeriac**

6 **spring onions**, finely sliced

2 tablespoons **sesame oil**

2 teaspoons **yellow mustard seeds**

1 tablespoon light **soy sauce**

2 tablespoons **lime juice**

pepper

Crisp carrots and nutty celeriac blend well with a mild peppery mustard dressing.

1 Cut the carrot and celeriac into thin julienne strips or grate them coarsely by hand. Place in a bowl with the spring onions.

2 Heat the oil gently in a small frying pan and add the mustard seeds. When they start to pop, remove the pan from the heat and add the seeds to the carrot and celeriac. (Be careful not to burn the mustard seeds or they will become bitter.)

3 Mix the soy sauce and lime juice in a small bowl, add plenty of pepper and pour over the salad. Toss well and serve.

500 g (1 lb) **baby corn cobs**, trimmed

2 tablespoons **sesame seeds**

6 **spring onions**, finely sliced

50 g (2 oz) **coriander**, chopped

50 ml (2 fl oz) **sunflower oil**

2 teaspoons **sesame oil**

2 tablespoons **lime juice** or **lemon juice**

1 tablespoon **soy sauce**

1–2 **red chillies**, deseeded and finely chopped (optional)

salt and **pepper**

crusty bread, to serve

PREP
20

COOK
6

SERVES
4–6

crunchy

Baby corn and spring onion salad

Crunchy little corn cobs in a dressing of spring onion, coriander and soy sauce make a deliciously memorable salad.

1   Bring a large saucepan of lightly salted water to the boil, add the corn and cook for 3–4 minutes until just tender. Drain in a colander, refresh under cold water and drain again well.

2   Place the sesame seeds in a dry frying pan. Heat, tossing, for 1–2 minutes, until evenly browned, then remove from the heat and set aside

3   Mix the rest of the ingredients in a salad bowl, add the corn cobs and toss lightly. Sprinkle with the toasted sesame seeds and serve with crusty bread.

Kohlrabi and bean sprout salad

This fresh, crisp salad combines crunchy bean sprouts and kohlrabi, a vegetable with a sweet, nutty flavour, sometimes called the cabbage-turnip.

1 Scatter the cashew nuts on a baking sheet and cook in a preheated oven, 180°C (350°F), Gas Mark 4, for 10–15 minutes until evenly golden. Leave to cool, then chop coarsely.

2 If using desiccated coconut, place in a bowl with warm water to cover. Leave to soak for 20 minutes, then strain through a sieve, pressing the coconut against the sides with the back of a spoon to squeeze out any excess moisture.

3 Peel the kohlrabi and grate it coarsely into a bowl. Add the bean sprouts, coconut, spring onions and mint, and mix well.

4 To make the dressing, mix together the garlic, lime juice and honey in a small bowl and pour over the salad. Toss lightly, then sprinkle with the toasted cashew nuts.

PREP
20*

COOK
15

SERVES
4–6

crisp

75 g (3 oz) **unsalted cashew nuts**

75 g (3 oz) **fresh coconut**, grated, or 50 g (2 oz) unsweetened **desiccated coconut**

250 g (8 oz) **kohlrabi**

125 g (4 oz) **bean sprouts**, rinsed and dried

3 **spring onions**, finely chopped

1 tablespoon chopped **mint**

1 **garlic clove**, crushed

2 tablespoons **lime juice**

2 tablespoons clear **honey**

* plus 20 minutes soaking, if using desiccated coconut

750 g (1½ lb) small **red potatoes**

125 g (4 oz) **feta cheese**, crumbled

CAPER VINAIGRETTE

1 tablespoon **sherry vinegar**

½ tablespoon **Dijon mustard**

2 tablespoons **capers**, drained and roughly chopped

1 tablespoon chopped **tarragon**

6 tablespoons **extra virgin olive oil**

salt and **pepper**

PREP
10

COOK
15

SERVES
4

spicy

Hot potato salad with feta and capers

This unusual and spicy vinaigrette, combined with hot rather than cold potatoes, transforms the classic potato salad into a completely new dish.

1 Cook the potatoes in a pan of lightly salted boiling water for 10–15 minutes until just tender. Drain and cut into bite-sized pieces, if necessary.

2 To make the caper vinaigrette, mix together the vinegar, mustard, capers and tarragon in a small bowl. Gradually whisk in the olive oil in a thin, steady stream until amalgamated, then season with salt and pepper.

3 Toss the warm potatoes with the vinaigrette and sprinkle with the feta before serving.

Couscous and celery salad

PREP
5*

SERVES
6

easy

This fragrant, herby salad is so easy to make and is delicious served with barbecued chicken or even spicy sausages.

1   Place the couscous in a bowl, add enough cold water to cover, then leave to stand for 30 minutes, until all the water has been absorbed.

2   Line a colander with muslin or a clean tea towel. Drain the couscous into the colander, then gather up the sides of the piece of muslin or the tea towel and squeeze to extract as much of the liquid as possible from the couscous. Tip the couscous into a salad bowl.

3   Stir in all the remaining ingredients apart from half of the lemon juice. Add salt and pepper to taste. Cover and set aside for 30 minutes, then taste the salad and add more lemon juice if required.

250 g (8 oz) quick-cooking **couscous**

6 **celery** sticks, very finely sliced

1 **red onion**, finely sliced

5 tablespoons chopped **mint**

5 tablespoons chopped **parsley**

2 teaspoons **fennel seeds**, crushed

2 tablespoons **olive oil**

finely grated rind and juice of 2 **lemons**

salt and **pepper**

* plus 30 minutes
soaking and
30 minutes standing

side dishes

500 g (1 lb) **new potatoes**, skins left on

4 long sprigs of **rosemary**

1 tablespoon **olive oil**

1 tablespoon **sea salt flakes**

PREP
5

COOK
20

SERVES
4

herby

Rosemary potatoes

This is a delicious potato recipe to serve with fish, poultry or meat – especially lamb, which goes so well with rosemary.

1 Boil the potatoes in a pan of lightly salted water for 10 minutes, then leave to cool.

2 Thread the potatoes on to the sprigs of rosemary, brush them with olive oil and sprinkle with sea salt.

3 Cook on an oiled barbecue grill over medium-hot coals for 10 minutes, turning occasionally.

Hasselback potatoes

PREP
5

COOK
25

SERVES
4

simple

16 small **new potatoes**

3 tablespoons **olive oil**

sea salt flakes

Simple yet so delicious, kids will love eating their potatoes from a stick. For the adults, try skewering the potatoes on rosemary stalks.

1   Divide the potatoes between 4 skewers. Using a small sharp knife, make thin slashes across each potato, then brush all the potatoes with the olive oil and sprinkle with some sea salt flakes.

2   Cook the potato skewers on an oiled barbecue grill over hot coals for 20–25 minutes.

750 g (1½ lb) **red potatoes**

6 **garlic cloves**, skins on

3 tablespoons **olive oil**

2 tablespoons chopped **rosemary**

rock salt and **pepper**

PREP
10

COOK
40

SERVES
4

golden

Garlic and rosemary fat chips

Serve these chunky chips with a salsa of choice, mayonnaise or for an extra garlicky taste try aïoli (see page 241).

1   Cut the potatoes into thick chips and put them in a large nonstick roasting tin. Crush the garlic cloves in their skins and scatter them over the chips. Drizzle with the olive oil and season with rosemary, rock salt and pepper. Cook in a preheated oven, 200°C (400°F), Gas Mark 6, for 40 minutes, giving the chips a good shake every 10 minutes to prevent them from sticking.

2   When the chips are crisp and golden, remove them from the oven, drain on kitchen paper and serve immediately.

Potato skins with soured cream

This recipe is equally delicious with sweet potatoes. Choose those with orange flesh, as they are prettier.

PREP
15

COOK
90

MAKES
20

creamy

5 large **baking potatoes**, scrubbed and dried

150 ml (¼ pint) **soured cream**

1 teaspoon snipped **chives**

vegetable oil, for brushing

salt and **pepper**

1 Prick the potatoes with a fork and bake them in a preheated oven, 190°C (375°F), Gas Mark 5, for about 1¼ hours until tender.

2 Meanwhile, mix the soured cream with the chives and salt and pepper to taste. Spoon into a bowl, cover and chill.

3 Leave the potatoes to cool for a few minutes, then cut each one in half lengthways, then again to make 4 long pieces. Using a teaspoon, scoop out most of the potato, leaving just a thin layer next to the skin. (Use the potato flesh in another dish.)

4 Brush the potato skins with oil, then cook them on an oiled barbecue grill over hot coals for 5–7 minutes on each side until golden. Sprinkle lightly with salt and serve with the soured cream dip.

4 large **potatoes,** scrubbed

8 **sun-dried tomatoes** in oil, drained and finely chopped

1 quantity **Aïoli** (see page 241)

4 tablespoons **olive oil**

paprika

sea salt flakes and **pepper**

PREP
10

COOK
25

SERVES
4

crispy

Barbecued potato wedges with aïoli

To make cooking and turning easier, thread the potato wedges on to wooden or metal skewers.

1 Place the whole, unpeeled potatoes in a large pan of cold water and bring to the boil, then reduce the heat and simmer for 15–20 minutes or until just tender. Drain, and when cool enough to handle, cut each potato into large wedges.

2 To make the sun-dried tomato aïoli, stir the sun-dried tomatoes into the aïoli.

3 Brush the potato wedges with the oil, sprinkle with a little paprika and put the potato wedges on an oiled barbecue grill. Cook over medium-hot coals for 5–6 minutes, turning frequently, until golden brown all over. Sprinkle with sea salt and serve with the aïoli.

Chilli potato wedges

Use as little or as much chilli powder as you like, to coat these oven-roasted potato wedges.

1 Cut each potato into 8 wedges and place in a large bowl. Add the oil, salt and chilli powder and toss until evenly coated.

2 Transfer the potatoes to a baking sheet and roast in a preheated oven, 220°C (425°F), Gas Mark 7, for 15 minutes. Turn them over and then cook for a further 15 minutes. Turn once more and cook for a final 25–30 minutes until crisp and golden.

3 Allow the potato wedges to cool slightly, then serve them with a spicy dip.

PREP
5

COOK
60

MAKES
32

hot

4 large **baking potatoes**

4–6 tablespoons **olive oil**

½ teaspoon **salt**

1–2 teaspoons **chilli powder**, to taste

spicy dip, to serve

2 **sweet potatoes**, finely sliced

4 tablespoons **cornflour**

2 tablespoons **Cajun seasoning**

vegetable oil, for deep-frying

PREP
10

COOK
10

SERVES
4

sweet

Cajun sweet potato chips

Hot sweet potato chips are comforting and warming – perfect for a Halloween barbecue or children's party.

1 Put the sweet potato slices in a large bowl with the cornflour and Cajun seasoning. Toss together well to coat the chips lightly.

2 Quarter-fill a large pan with vegetable oil and heat it to 180°C (350°F), or until a piece of bread browns in 30 seconds. Fry the potatoes in batches for 2 minutes until golden and crisp. Drain on plenty of kitchen paper.

Grilled sweet potato slices with aïoli

Serve with pork steaks and crisp salad leaves or green beans.

1   Brush the sweet potatoes with the olive oil and cook on an oiled barbecue grill over medium-hot coals for about 5 minutes on each side until tender.

2   Serve hot with the aïoli.

PREP
15

COOK
10

SERVES
4

garlicky

500 g (1 lb) **sweet potatoes**, scrubbed and cut into 5 mm (¼ inch slices)

4 tablespoons **olive oil**

1 quantity **Aïoli** (see page 241)

2 large **parsnips**

1 teaspoon **dried thyme**

1 tablespoon **plain flour**

vegetable oil, for deep-frying

PREP
10

COOK
10

SERVES
4

toasted

Straw parsnip chips with thyme

These chips can also be roasted if you prefer, and fresh thyme can be used instead of the dried thyme.

1 Slice the parsnips very thinly, preferably using a mandolin with a thin julienne blade. Dry them on kitchen paper, then put them in a bowl and toss with the dried thyme and flour.

2 Quarter-fill a large pan with vegetable oil and heat to 180°C (350°F), or until a piece of bread browns in 30 seconds. Fry the parsnips in batches for 2 minutes or until golden and crisp. Drain on lots of kitchen paper.

Pumpkin wedges with coconut pesto

Creamy coconut pesto makes a perfect foil to the soft, nutty wedges of barbecued pumpkin dusted with curry spices.

1 Cut the pumpkin into thin wedges about 1 cm (½ inch) thick, leaving the skin on, and place in a large dish.

2 Put the whole spices in a frying pan and dry-fry until browned, then grind to a powder in a spice grinder. Mix with the oil and sugar or mango chutney and toss with the pumpkin wedges to coat.

3 Cook the wedges on an oiled barbecue grill over hot coals for 6–8 minutes on each side, until charred and tender.

4 Meanwhile, to make the pesto, put the coriander leaves, garlic, chilli, sugar and nuts into a food processor. Whizz until fairly finely ground and blended. Season to taste with salt and pepper. Add the coconut cream and lime juice and whizz again. Transfer the pesto to a serving bowl and serve with the pumpkin wedges.

PREP
15

COOK
20

SERVES
4

spicy

1 kg (2 lb) **pumpkin**

1 teaspoon **cumin seeds**

1 teaspoon **coriander seeds**

2 **cardamom pods**

3 tablespoons **sunflower oil**

1 teaspoon **caster sugar** or **mango chutney**

COCONUT PESTO

25 g (1 oz) **coriander leaves**

1 **garlic clove**, crushed

1 **green chilli**, deseeded and chopped

pinch of **sugar**

1 tablespoon shelled **pistachio nuts**, roughly chopped

6 tablespoons **coconut cream**

1 tablespoon **lime juice**

salt and **pepper**

3 **onions**, cut into 1 cm (¼ inch) rings

500 ml (17 fl oz) **buttermilk**

125 g (4 oz) **plain flour**

2 teaspoons sweet or ordinary **paprika**

1 teaspoon **cayenne pepper**

1 teaspoon freshly ground **pepper**

1 teaspoon **rock salt**

vegetable oil, for deep-frying

PREP
15*

COOK
10

SERVES
4

crunchy

Southern fried onion rings

When buying the buttermilk, go for one that is the consistency of pouring double cream. If you can't find sweet paprika, ordinary paprika will do fine for this recipe.

1 Place the onion rings in a large bowl and pour over the buttermilk. Leave to marinate for at least 30 minutes.

2 Mix together the remaining ingredients on a large plate.

3 Quarter-fill a large pan with vegetable oil and heat to 180°C (350°F), or until a piece of bread browns in 30 seconds.

4 Remove a small handful of onion rings from the buttermilk and coat in the seasoned flour. Cook the rings in the oil for 2 minutes or until golden brown, then drain well on kitchen paper. Repeat until all the onion rings are cooked, and serve warm.

* plus 30 minutes marinating

Olives with an Asian flavour

PREP
5

SERVES
8

oriental

Kaffir lime leaves have a pungent flavour; they can be found in large international supermarkets or Asian stores.

1   Place the olives in a bowl, add the remaining ingredients and stir well.

2   Cover and refrigerate for up to 1 week.

250 g (8 oz) mixed **green** and **black olives**

1 **garlic clove**, crushed

1 teaspoon grated **ginger**

2 **kaffir lime leaves**, shredded or the grated rind of 1 **lime**

2 **red chillies**, bruised

2 tablespoons dark **soy sauce**

4 tablespoons **extra virgin olive oil**

6 sheets **filo pastry**, 31 x 21 cm (12½ x 8½ inches), defrosted if frozen

75 g (3 oz) **butter**, melted

175 g (6 oz) **Emmenthal cheese**, finely grated

PREP
10

COOK
15

MAKES
22

crisp

Filo and Emmenthal wafers

These crisp savoury wafers make excellent biscuits to serve with drinks and dips, and can be stored in an airtight container for 3–4 days.

1 Lightly brush 1 sheet of filo pastry with butter and scatter with a little of the cheese. Put a second sheet on top, brush with melted butter and scatter with more cheese. Repeat with a third sheet, finishing with the cheese. Do the same with the remaining 3 sheets of filo pastry so that you have 2 stacks of pastry.

2 Using a 7.5 cm (3 inch) plain round pastry cutter, cut the filo layers into circles and place them on a heavy baking sheet. Alternatively, cut the pastry into rectangular 10 x 3 cm (4 x 1¼ inch) wafers, in which case you will get 42.

3 Bake the wafers in a preheated oven, 180°C (350°F), Gas Mark 4, for 15 minutes until crisp and light brown. Remove from the baking sheet and cool on a wire rack.

Seeded cheese sablés

Serve these crisp savoury biscuits with dips, soup, crudités, and roasted or grilled vegetables.

PREP
20*

COOK
12

MAKES
ABOUT
30

hot

1 Put the flour, butter, mustard, cayenne and salt in a food processor and whizz until the mixture resembles fine breadcrumbs. Add the Cheddar and continue to whizz for a few seconds until the mixture begins to come together to make a soft dough.

2 Turn the mixture out on to a lightly floured surface and knead gently. Wrap in clingfilm and chill for about 30 minutes.

3 Roll out the pastry on a lightly floured surface to about 2.5 mm (⅛ inch) thick. Cut it into circles using a 6 cm (2½ inch) fluted pastry cutter. Knead the trimmings together, roll them out and cut out more circles.

4 Line 2 heavy baking sheets with nonstick baking paper and place the sablés on them. Sprinkle with Parmesan and dust with mustard and poppy seeds. Bake in a preheated oven, 200°C (400°F), Gas Mark 6, for 9–12 minutes until crisp and light golden. Transfer to a wire rack with a palette knife. Serve hot, or set aside to cool and store in an airtight container to serve later.

125 g (4 oz) **plain flour**

75 g (3 oz) **unsalted butter**, cut into small pieces

1 tablespoon **English mustard powder**

pinch of **cayenne pepper**

pinch of **salt**

125 g (4 oz) mature **Cheddar cheese**, finely grated

40–50 g (1½–2 oz) **Parmesan cheese**, finely grated

2 tablespoons **black mustard seeds**

1 tablespoon **poppy seeds**

125 g (4 oz) mature farmhouse or vegetarian **Cheddar, Gruyère** or **raclette cheese**, coarsely grated or diced

Cheesy crisps

PREP
10

COOK
10

MAKES
8–10

bubbly

These can be served as a savoury with drinks, or as an accompaniment to salsas and dips of your choice.

1   Line several baking sheets with nonstick baking paper. Place 2 mounds of cheese on each sheet, no more than 8 cm (3⅛ inches) in diameter and at least 10 cm (4 inches) apart. As it cooks, the cheese will spread to form rough biscuit shapes.

2   Bake the crisps in a preheated oven, 220°C (425°F), Gas Mark 7, for 10 minutes until the cheese bubbles and begins to turn a very pale cream. If it turns too golden, the crisps will taste bitter.

3   Allow the crisps to cool slightly, then transfer them with a spatula to a wire rack to cool completely. Serve at once or store as required.

Pitta chips

PREP
10

COOK
15

MAKES
48

tasty

6 **white pitta breads**

3 **garlic cloves**, crushed

1 tablespoon **dried mixed herbs**

6 tablespoons **olive oil**

2 teaspoons **mild chilli powder**

2 teaspoons **paprika**

dips, to serve

A simple way to spice up pitta breads. If your pittas aren't that fresh they will be given a new lease of life with this recipe.

1 Split open the pittas, then cut each half into quarters. Divide them equally between 2 large roasting tins. In the first tin rub the garlic, mixed herbs and half the olive oil, into the bread. Rub the chilli powder, paprika and the remaining oil into the second batch of bread.

2 Bake the pittas in a preheated oven, 200°C (400°F), Gas Mark 6, for 15 minutes or until lightly golden in colour and crispy. Serve warm or cold with a selection of dips.

4 thick slices of day-old **country-style bread**

2 **garlic cloves**, halved

extra virgin olive oil, to drizzle

TOPPING

1 **yellow pepper**, cored, deseeded and quartered

1 **red pepper**, cored, deseeded and quartered

2 tablespoons **hazelnut oil**

2 **garlic cloves**, sliced

1 tablespoon grated **lemon rind**

25 g (1 oz) **sultanas**

25 g (1 oz) **flaked hazelnuts**

175 g (6 oz) **salad leaves** (such as baby spinach, rocket, frisée)

PREP
10

COOK
15

SERVES
4

nutty

Bruschetta with peppers and hazelnuts

The sultanas and peppers provide a sweet, colourful topping to this classic Italian starter.

1 To make the topping, grill the pepper quarters, skin side down, on an oiled barbecue grill over hot coals for 6–8 minutes until charred and tender. Place them in a plastic bag, seal and set aside until the peppers are cool enough to handle. Peel off the skin and slice the flesh.

2 Heat the hazelnut oil in a frying pan, add the garlic, lemon rind, sultanas and hazelnuts and fry gently for 5 minutes until golden. Add the salad leaves and cook over a low heat for 3 minutes, or until just wilted.

3 Meanwhile, prepare the bruschetta. Toast the bread lightly on both sides on the barbecue grill rack. Immediately rub the toast all over with the garlic cloves and drizzle with olive oil.

4 Divide the salad mixture between the bruschetta and top with the grilled peppers. Serve at once.

Grissini

PREP
20*

COOK
8

MAKES
16–20

salty

Nothing like the ones in packets, these grissini are fun to make and great served with drinks as the barbecue heats up.

1 To prepare the yeast, follow the instructions on the easy-blend yeast packet.

2 Sift the flour into a large bowl and make a well in the centre. Pour in the yeast mixture, olive oil and salt. Mix together with a round-bladed knife, then with your hand, until the dough comes together.

3 Tip the dough out on to a floured surface. Wash and dry your hands, then knead the dough for about 10 minutes until it is smooth and elastic. Place it in a clean, oiled bowl, cover with a damp tea towel and leave to rise until doubled in size. This will take about an hour.

4 Working on a well-floured work surface, roll out the dough thinly to make a rectangle. Cut it into 5 mm (¼ inch) strips, following the long side of the rectangle. Lightly roll out these strips and taper the ends.

5 Brush the grissini lightly with water and sprinkle with the flavouring of your choice. Put them on a baking sheet and bake in a preheated oven, 200°C (400°F), Gas Mark 6, for 5–8 minutes until crisp and brown. Leave to cool completely.

6 To serve, twist strips of prosciutto around a bunch of grissini.

2 sachets **easy-blend dried yeast**

pinch of **sugar**

125 ml (4 fl oz) warm **water**

175 g (6 oz) **Italian flour**

1 tablespoon **olive oil**

1 teaspoon coarse **sea salt**

slices of **prosciutto**, cut into strips, to serve

FLAVOURINGS

coarse **sea salt**

sesame seeds

poppy seeds

cracked black **pepper**

Naan bread

1 teaspoon **easy-blend dried yeast**

1 teaspoon **caster sugar**

50 ml (2 fl oz) warm **milk**

250 g (8 oz) **plain flour**

½ teaspoon **salt**

1 tablespoon **vegetable oil**

1 **egg**, beaten

4 tablespoons **natural yogurt**

PREP
20*

COOK
25

SERVES
4

warm

Naan bread is so easy to make and it is far more delicious than anything you can buy. If you fancy a change, sprinkle the naans with coriander and butter before grilling.

1 Sprinkle the yeast and sugar over the warm milk. Mix, cover and keep warm for 15–20 minutes until frothy.

2 Sift the flour and salt into a large bowl, make a well in the centre and add the rest of the ingredients plus the yeast mixture. Mix together, gradually incorporating the flour until the dough forms a soft ball. Turn out on to a floured work surface, knead for 10 minutes until smooth, then place in an oiled bowl. Cover and leave to rise in a warm place for 1 hour or until the dough has doubled in size.

3 Return the dough to the floured surface, punch it down to remove the air, then knead for 5 minutes more. Divide it into 4 portions, roll each one into 20 x 12 cm (8 x 5 inch) tear shapes and place them on an oiled baking sheet. Cover and leave to rise for 25 minutes in a warm place.

4 Heat a cast-iron pan and cook each piece of dough for 3 minutes. Then place them under a grill for 2–3 minutes, until golden and spotty on top.

* plus 1½ hours
proving

Sun-dried tomato and olive focaccia

Eat the focaccia the same day they are made or freeze as soon as they have cooled. This recipe makes two thin 25 cm (10 inch) loaves. Wash and dry your hands before you knead the dough.

1 Follow the packet instructions for easy-blend yeast. Sift the flour into a large bowl and make a well. Pour in the yeast mixture and 3 tablespoons of the olive oil. Mix with a round-bladed knife, then your hands, until the dough comes together.

2 Tip out the dough on to a floured surface. Knead it for 10 minutes until smooth and elastic. Place in a clean, oiled bowl, cover with a damp cloth and leave to rise in a warm place until doubled – about 1½ hours.

3 Lightly oil two shallow 25 cm (10 inch) pie tins. Knock down the dough and knead in the sun-dried tomatoes, capers and half the olives. Divide the dough in half. Working on a floured surface, shape each piece into a round and roll out to a 25 cm (10 inch) circle. Place them on the tins, cover with a damp cloth and leave to rise for 30 minutes.

4 Remove the tea towel and make dimples all over the surface of the dough with your fingertips. They can be quite deep. Cover the dough again and leave to rise until doubled in size – about 2 hours.

5 Pour over the remaining oil, scatter with the rest of the olives and sprinkle with salt. Spray the dough with water, then bake in a preheated oven, 200°C (400°F), Gas Mark 6, for 20–25 minutes. Transfer to a wire rack to cool.

PREP
25*

COOK
25

MAKES
2

fresh

1 sachet **easy-blend dried yeast**

pinch of **sugar**

450 ml (¾ pint) warm **water**

750 g (1½ lb) **plain flour**, plus extra for dusting

125 ml (4 fl oz) good **olive oil**

50 g (2 oz) **sun-dried tomatoes** (the dried kind), soaked and sliced

2 tablespoons **salted capers**, rinsed

250 g (8 oz) **black** or **green olives**, pitted

coarse **sea salt**

* plus 4 hours proving

STARTER DOUGH

¼ teaspoon **dry active yeast**

250 ml (8 fl oz) warm **water**

375 g (12 oz) **strong white flour**

½ teaspoon **sugar**

BREAD DOUGH

1½ teaspoons **dry active yeast**

900 ml (1½ pints) **warm water**

1 teaspoon **sugar**

750 g (1½ lb) **strong white flour**

250 g (8 oz) **semolina**, plus extra for sprinkling

1½ tablespoons **salt**

PREP
40*

COOK
30

MAKES
2

tasty

Sourdough bread

This bread needs planning in advance as it takes several days to prepare. It is well worth the wait, especially when served warm with a steak.

1 Four days before making the bread, prepare the starter dough. Stir the yeast into the warm water. Add about 4 tablespoons of the flour and the sugar; leave to froth for 10 minutes. Work the mixture into the remaining flour; cover with clingfilm. Leave in a warm place for at least 3 days.

2 Dissolve the yeast in 150 ml (¼ pint) of the warm water, add the sugar and 4 tablespoons of the flour and leave to froth for 10 minutes. Transfer to a large bowl and gradually work in 125 g (4 oz) of the starter dough (chill the rest and use as required), the remaining warm water and flour, the semolina and salt until a sticky, slightly lumpy dough. Transfer the dough to an oiled bowl, cover with oiled clingfilm and leave in a warm place for several hours to double in size.

3 Tip out the dough on to a floured surface, cut off about 125 g (4 oz) and add it to the starter mixture. Halve the remaining dough and shape each piece into a flat round. Roll up the dough, turn it 180° and repeat the rolling. Transfer to a well-floured baking sheet, sprinkle with semolina and cover with a clean cloth. Leave to rise for 1–2 hours, until doubled.

4 Score the surface with a knife and bake in a preheated oven, 230°C (450°F), Gas Mark 8, for 30 minutes. Cool on a wire rack.

* plus 3 days for the starter and many hours proving

Griddle bread

COOK
4

MAKES
8

easy

500 g (1 lb) **plain flour**

250 g (8 oz) **wholemeal flour**

2 teaspoons **salt**

1 teaspoon **fast-acting yeast**

450 ml (¾ pint) warm **water**

1 tablespoon **extra virgin olive oil**, plus extra for brushing

These individual breads take just a couple of minutes to cook. Split them down one side and fill with falafels and salad.

1 Sift the flours and salt into the bowl of a food mixer. Stir in the yeast and then, with the dough hook turning, gradually add the water and oil to form a soft dough. Knead for 8–10 minutes, until smooth and elastic.

2 Transfer the dough to an oiled bowl, cover with a tea towel and leave to rise in a warm place for 1 hour, until doubled in size.

3 Divide the dough into 8 pieces and roll out each one on a lightly floured surface to form an oval (about the same size as commercial pitta breads), brush with a little oil and leave to rise for about 10 minutes.

4 Heat a griddle or heavy-based pan until really hot and cook the breads in batches for about 2 minutes on each side, until spotted with brown and puffed up. Serve immediately.

desserts

1–2 tablespoons **caster sugar**

½ teaspoon **ground cinnamon**

2 teaspoons **rum**

250 g (8 oz) **mascarpone cheese**

8 small **bananas**

Bananas and mascarpone cream

Bananas change their texture and taste completely different when barbecued, becoming meltingly tender and very sweet.

1 Mix the sugar, cinnamon and rum in a bowl. Stir in the mascarpone, mix well and set aside.

2 Cook the whole, unpeeled bananas on a barbecue grill over hot coals for 10–12 minutes, turning the bananas as the skins darken, until they are black all over and the flesh is very tender.

3 To serve, split the bananas open and spread the flesh with the flavoured mascarpone.

Barbecued fruits with palm sugar

Soft, sweet and syrupy – the perfect end to a barbecue. Squeeze the lime over the top of the fruit and serve with plenty of ice cream.

1 Warm the sugar, lime rind and juice, measurement water and peppercorns together in a small pan until the sugar has dissolved. Plunge the base of the pan into iced water to cool.

2 Brush the cooled syrup over the prepared fruits, then cook on an oiled barbecue grill over medium-hot coals for 3–4 minutes on each side until charred and tender.

3 Serve with scoops of cinnamon or vanilla ice cream and slices of lime.

PREP
10

COOK
8

SERVES
4

exotic

25 g (1 oz) **palm sugar**

grated rind and juice of 1 **lime**

2 tablespoons **water**

½ teaspoon cracked **black peppercorns**

500 g (1 lb) mixed prepared **fruits** (such as pineapple slices, mango wedges and peach halves)

TO SERVE

cinnamon or **vanilla ice cream**

slices of **lime**

1 kg (2 lb) assorted **fruits** in season (e.g. mango, papaya, peach, strawberries, oranges, apples or pears)

lime or **lemon juice**, for brushing

double cream, **mascarpone cheese** or **yogurt**, to serve (optional)

RUM BUTTER GLAZE

75 g (3 oz) **butter**

2 tablespoons **muscovado sugar**

1 tablespoon **rum** or a **liqueur** of **your choice**

PREP
25

COOK
7

SERVES
4

glossy

Fruit skewers with rum butter glaze

For the best results, choose varieties of fruit that will take roughly the same length of time to cook.

1 To make the rum butter glaze, melt the butter in a small saucepan together with the muscovado sugar. Stir in the rum or a liqueur of your choice.

2 Prepare the fruit according to type and cut it into bite-sized pieces. Thread the pieces on to 8 skewers, alternating the different types of fruit to create a colourful effect.

3 Brush all the fruit with lime or lemon juice and then brush them with the flavoured butter glaze. Cook on an oiled barbecue grill over medium-hot coals for 2–3 minutes on each side, brush with more butter and then cook the skewers for 1 minute more.

4 Serve the hot grilled skewers at once, together with a separate bowl of cream, mascarpone, or yogurt for dipping, if liked.

Grilled honeyed peaches

Sweet, fragrant peaches served hot from the grill with a Marsala syrup and crunchy amaretti biscuits make a very simple but spectacular dessert.

1 Cut a small cross in the top and bottom of each peach and place it in a pan of boiling water. Leave for 20 seconds, then transfer with a slotted spoon to a bowl of cold water. Peel, cut in half lengthways and remove the stone.

2 Place the Marsala, honey and orange rind in a small saucepan, bring to the boil, then reduce the heat and simmer for 2 minutes. Add the peach halves and simmer for 3–4 minutes until just tender. Remove the pan from the heat and leave the peaches to cool in the syrup.

3 Remove the peaches with a slotted spoon and place the remaining syrup in a small pan. Bring to the boil and reduce by half.

4 Brush the peaches with the melted butter, then cook on a barbecue grill over medium-hot coals for 5–7 minutes, turning once.

5 Transfer the hot peaches to serving plates, spoon over a little of the reduced syrup and crumble over the amaretti biscuits. Serve with vanilla ice cream or crème fraîche.

PREP
15

COOK
20

SERVES
4

simple

4 ripe **peaches**

300 ml (½ pint) **Marsala**

4 tablespoons **honey**

1 strip of **orange rind**

25 g (1 oz) **butter**, melted

4 **amaretti biscuits**

vanilla ice cream or **crème fraîche**, to serve

12 ripe **figs**

125 g (4 oz) **blackberries**

pared rind and juice of
2 **oranges**

2 tablespoons **crème de
cassis**

1 tablespoon **caster sugar**

½ teaspoon **cinnamon**

25 g (1 oz) **butter**, melted

4 slices **brioche** or **white
bread**

fromage frais or **Greek
yogurt**, to serve (optional)

PREP
10

COOK
10

SERVES
4

unusual

Figs and blackberries on toast

Hot, squidgy figs and blackberries baked in liqueur are served with crispy cinnamon brioche toast to mop up the delicious cooking juices.

1 Cut the figs into quarters, slicing them almost but not all the way through, so the quarters fall back like flower petals. Cut 4 squares of double-thickness foil and place 3 figs and a quarter of the blackberries on each one.

2 Cut the orange rind into thin julienne strips and put in a bowl. Stir in the orange juice and crème de cassis and divide between the fig parcels. Bring up the edges of the foil and press to seal.

3 Mix the sugar, cinnamon and melted butter in a bowl and brush over one side of each brioche or bread slice.

4 Cook the fig parcels on a barbecue grill over medium-hot coals for about 8–10 minutes, or until the figs are hot and slightly soft. Towards the end of the cooking time, add the buttered brioche or bread slices to the grill and toast until golden.

5 Serve the cinnamon toasts on individual plates, topped with the figs and blackberries. Add a spoonful of fromage frais or Greek yogurt, if liked.

Rum-flambéed pineapple parcels

PREP
15

COOK
18

SERVES
4

buttery

1 ripe **pineapple**, peeled

50 g (2 oz) **butter**

75 g (3 oz) **light muscovado sugar**

4 tablespoons dark **rum** (optional)

50 g (2 oz) **pecan nuts**, toasted and coarsely chopped

crème fraîche, to serve

Muscovado is a raw sugar obtained from sugar cane juice; if you can't find it in the supermarket use ordinary brown sugar instead.

1 Cut the pineapple into 8 even slices, then remove the cores with a small pastry cutter to make rings.

2 Cut 4 squares of double-thickness foil, each large enough to hold 2 pineapple rings in a loose parcel. Place 2 rings on each square.

3 Melt the butter in a small saucepan, stir in the sugar and cook gently until the sugar has dissolved. Divide it between the parcels, then bring the edges of the foil together and press to seal. Cook on a barbecue grill rack over medium-hot coals for 10–15 minutes.

4 When the pineapple is cooked, open the packages carefully, spoon 1 tablespoon of rum into each one and set alight with a long match, if liked. Scatter with the chopped pecans and serve at once with crème fraîche.

750 g (1½ lb) **blueberries**

6–8 tablespoons **vanilla sugar**

6–8 tablespoons **crème de cassis**

single cream, to serve (optional)

ALMOND CREAM

750 g (1½ lb) **ground almonds**

1 kg (2 lb) **mascarpone cheese**

3 **egg yolks**

100 g (3½ oz) **caster sugar**

125 ml (4 fl oz) **double cream**

2 tablespoons **Amaretto**

PREP
15*

COOK
10

SERVES
6–8

nutty

Blueberry parcels with almond cream

A little fiddly but a great recipe if you have just a few people to cater for and you want to impress. Make the almond cream the night before.

1 To make the almond cream, first line an 18 cm (7 inch) sieve with a piece of muslin large enough to overhang the edge by about 10 cm (4 inches). Place the lined sieve over a bowl. In a mixing bowl, beat the ground almonds with the mascarpone. In a separate bowl, beat the egg yolks with the sugar until pale and fluffy. Fold the egg mixture into the mascarpone mixture.

2 Whip the cream in another bowl until it forms soft peaks. Fold into the mascarpone with the Amaretto. Turn the mixture into the lined sieve, fold the excess muslin over, cover with a small plate and set a small weight on top. Place in the refrigerator for 6–8 hours or overnight, to drain.

3 Cut 6–8 x 33 cm (13 inch) squares of double-thickness foil. Heap a quarter of the blueberries in the centre of each foil square and turn up the edges of the foil to form a lip. Sprinkle the blueberries with 1 tablespoon of the vanilla sugar and drizzle with 1 tablespoon of the crème de cassis. Bring up the edges of the foil to make a parcel and press together to seal. Cook the sealed foil parcels on a barbecue grill over medium-hot coals for 8–10 minutes.

4 Unmould the almond cream on to a large plate. Serve portions of the cream beside the blueberries with a jug of single cream, if liked.

* plus 6–8 hours draining

Fresh blueberry cheesecake

This classic dessert never fails to please and, with little cooking to do, it couldn't be easier. Raspberries or strawberries could be used as they are a good alternative to blueberries.

1 To make the biscuit base, mix the biscuit crumbs in a bowl with the caster sugar and allspice. Melt the butter and jam together in a small saucepan, then stir into the crumb mixture. Press into the bottom and up the sides of a greased and lined 20 cm (8 inch) springform cake tin. Refrigerate.

2 Place the sugar in a saucepan with the water and heat gently to dissolve the sugar. Add half of the blueberries and simmer gently for 2 minutes. Remove from the heat and leave to cool.

3 To make the filling, dissolve the gelatine in the orange juice in a large bowl set over a saucepan of simmering water. Stir in the brown sugar and orange rind. Add the cream cheese and ricotta and beat thoroughly. Reserve a little cream and fold the rest into the filling.

4 Strain the cooked blueberries. Spread them over the biscuit base, cover with the cheese filling, and top with the remaining blueberries and cream. Chill for 5–6 hours.

PREP
20*

COOK
5

SERVES
8

creamy

1 tablespoon **sugar**

1 tablespoon **water**

250 g (8 oz) **blueberries**

BISCUIT BASE

125 g (4 oz) **digestive biscuits**, crushed

75 g (3 oz) **caster sugar**

1 teaspoon **ground allspice**

75 g (3 oz) **butter**

1½ tablespoons **apricot jam**

FILLING

1 tablespoon **powdered gelatine**

125 ml (4 fl oz) **orange juice**

150 g (5 oz) **light brown sugar**

2 tablespoons grated **orange rind**

425 g (14 oz) **cream cheese**

425 g (14 oz) **ricotta**

125 ml (4 fl oz) **double cream**, whipped

375 g (12 oz) **dark chocolate**, at least 50% cocoa solids, broken into squares

2 tablespoons **water**

175 ml (6 fl oz) **double cream**

75 g (3 oz) **unsalted butter**

1–2 tablespoons **rum**

75 g (3 oz) good-quality **candied peel** (optional)

fruit, to serve

PRALINE

125 g (4 oz) **caster sugar**

125 g (4 oz) whole **blanched almonds**

PREP
20*

SERVES
6–8

rich

Chocolate and praline truffle terrine

A sweet terrine makes a great party dessert. This one can be sliced to serve 20 and is delicious with fresh fruit and pouring cream.

1 Grease and line a 20 x 10 cm (8 x 4 inch) loaf tin with nonstick baking paper, and oil a baking sheet.

2 To make the praline, combine the sugar and almonds in a small, heavy saucepan. Heat gently until the sugar melts, stirring often. Continue to cook, stirring occasionally, until the sugar turns a deep golden brown and registers 165°C (330°F) on a sugar thermometer. Immediately remove from the heat and pour on to the oiled baking sheet, spreading it out slightly. Leave to cool. When the praline is completely cold, crush it into small pieces.

3 Melt the broken chocolate with the measurement water in a heatproof bowl over a saucepan of barely simmering water. Remove from the heat and leave to cool slightly.

4 Whip the cream in a bowl until it forms soft peaks. In a separate bowl, cream the butter until soft and fluffy, then slowly stir in the chocolate mixture, followed by the rum. Fold in the cream, crushed praline and the candied peel, if using. Pour the mixture into the lined loaf tin. Level the top, cover and place in the refrigerator for 2–3 hours.

5 To serve, unmould the terrine on to a platter and cut into thin slices. Serve seasonal fresh fruits as an accompaniment.

* plus 2–3 hours chilling

Coffee meringues

PREP
40

COOK
90

SERVES
6

crunchy

These meringues can be served with espresso coffee, or sandwich them together with whipped cream, nuts and flaked chocolate for a filling dessert.

1 Line 2 baking sheets with nonstick baking paper. Draw 6 x 7.5 cm (3 inch) circles and 6 x 5 cm (2 inch) circles on the paper with a pencil.

2 Whisk the egg whites until stiff, then whisk in the sugar 1 tablespoon at a time. Add the coffee powder and continue whisking until the meringue is very stiff and holds its shape.

3 Spoon into a piping bag fitted with a 1 cm (⅛ inch) plain nozzle and pipe over the rounds.

4 Bake in a preheated oven, 110°C (225°F), Gas Mark ⅛, for 1½ hours until crisp. Peel the paper carefully off the meringues, then cool on a rack.

5 Whip together the cream and liqueur in a bowl until stiff. Spoon into a piping bag fitted with a large fluted nozzle and pipe three-quarters of the cream on to the larger meringue circles.

6 Top with the small circles, then pipe a whirl on each one with the remaining cream to serve. Decorate with toasted pistachios or almonds.

MERINGUES

2 **egg whites**

125 g (4 oz) **caster sugar**

1 tablespoon **instant coffee powder**

COFFEE CREAM FILLING

250–300 ml (8–10 fl oz) **double cream**

2 tablespoons **Tia Maria** or other **coffee-flavoured liqueur**

pistachios or **almonds**, toasted, to decorate

4 tablespoons very strong **espresso coffee**

2 tablespoons **grappa** or **brandy**

10 **sponge-finger biscuits**

125 g (4 oz) **raspberries**

175 g (6 oz) **mascarpone cheese**

2 **eggs**, separated

50 g (2 oz) **icing sugar**

25 g (1 oz) **plain chocolate**

mint leaves, to decorate

PREP
15*

SERVES
4

smooth

Tiramisu with raspberry surprise

This dessert is best made the night before so that it can set completely.

1 Combine the coffee and grappa or brandy. Dip the sponge fingers into the liquid to coat them evenly, then arrange them in a small, shallow dish or a serving platter, pouring any excess liquid over them. Sprinkle the raspberries evenly over the soaked sponge fingers.

2 In a bowl, whisk the mascarpone, egg yolks and icing sugar until smooth and well blended.

3 In another bowl, whisk the egg whites until stiff and glossy, then fold into the mascarpone mixture until well blended.

4 Spoon the mixture over the sponge fingers and smooth the surface. Finely grate the chocolate straight on to the mixture. Cover and chill for 2 hours, or until set. Decorate with mint leaves.

* plus 2 hours chilling

Raspberry sorbet

PREP
10*

COOK
10

SERVES
4–6

icy

500 g (1 lb) **raspberries**, fresh or frozen

125 g (4 oz) **sugar**

300 ml (½ pint) **water**

2 **egg whites**

For a special occasion, pour a little liqueur, such as Cointreau, cassis or framboise, over each serving.

1 Thaw the raspberries at room temperature for 3–4 hours if you are using them from the freezer. Pass the raspberries through a sieve.

2 Put the sugar and measurement water in a saucepan and stir over a gentle heat until the sugar has dissolved. Increase the heat and boil briskly, without stirring, for 8 minutes or until a syrup has formed. Allow to cool.

3 Stir the syrup into the raspberry purée and pour into an ice tray or shallow rigid container. Place in the freezer for 1 hour or until just smooth. Whisk the egg whites until stiff and fold into the raspberry mixture.

4 Thaw the sorbet in the refrigerator for around 10–15 minutes before serving.

* plus 1 hour
freezing

150 ml (¼ pint) **Champagne** or **dry sparkling wine**

2 tablespoons **caster sugar**

finely grated rind and juice of ½ **lemon**

300 ml (½ pint) **double cream**

ripe **strawberries**, to serve

PREP
10*

COOK
4

SERVES
4

tangy

Champagne syllabub with strawberries

For a special occasion, serve this dessert with a mixture of cultivated and wild strawberries.

1 Mix the Champagne, sugar, lemon rind and juice together in a large bowl.

2 Add the cream and whisk the mixture until it forms soft peaks. Spoon into glasses and chill for 1–2 hours. Serve with ripe strawberries.

* plus 1–2 hours chilling

Kissel of summer berries

Kissel is a Russian fruit dessert; it is thickened with arrowroot and is similar to a sweet soup. If you like, finish it with a swirl of soured cream.

PREP
30*

COOK
55

SERVES
6

fruity

1 Grease a 20 x 7 cm (8 x 3 inch) loaf tin and line it with nonstick baking paper. Whisk the eggs, sugar and vanilla essence until thick and creamy. Carefully fold in the flour and almonds, spoon into the loaf tin and level the top.

2 Bake the mixture in a preheated oven, 160°C (325°F), Gas Mark 3, for 30–35 minutes or until a skewer comes out clean. Cool slightly in the tin, then invert on to a rack to cool completely.

3 Cut the loaf into very thin slices and arrange in a single layer on a baking sheet. Bake in a preheated oven, 150°C (300°F), Gas Mark 2, for 15–20 minutes until lightly golden, then cool on wire racks.

4 Meanwhile, set aside 125 g (4 oz) of the fruit for decoration. Place the remaining fruit with the water in a saucepan. Bring to the boil, then turn off the heat and leave to cool slightly. Whizz in a food processor until smooth, then strain through a sieve into a clean saucepan to remove any pips or seeds.

5 Bring the purée to the boil. Whisk in the arrowroot paste, if using, with the sugar. When the purée thickens, pour it into a bowl and cover closely to prevent a skin forming. Cool, then chill.

6 Pour the kissel into soup plates and decorate with the reserved fruit. Serve with the almond biscuits.

500 g (1 lb) mixed **summer berries** (raspberries, strawberries, cherries and red, white or blackcurrants), prepared

600 ml (1 pint) **water**

1 tablespoon **arrowroot** mixed to a paste with 2 tablespoons water (optional)

3–4 tablespoons **sugar**

ALMOND BISCUITS

2 **eggs**

125 g (4 oz) **caster sugar**

½ teaspoon **vanilla essence**

125 g (4 oz) **plain flour**, sifted

125 g (4 oz) whole **blanched almonds**, toasted

750 g (1½ lb) **apricots**, halved and pitted

4 **eggs**, beaten

125 g (4 oz) **caster sugar**, plus extra for sprinkling

pinch of **salt**

50 g (2 oz) **plain flour**

250 ml (8 fl oz) **milk**

50 g (2 oz) **butter**

2 tablespoons **apricot brandy**

crème fraîche, to serve

PREP
15

COOK
40

SERVES
4–6

sweet

Apricot clafoutis

A slightly different version of the classic French dessert (usually made with cherries) is made here with fresh apricots in a sweetened batter.

1 Lightly grease a 28 x 18 cm (11 x 7 inch) shallow ovenproof dish. Arrange the apricot halves cut side up in the dish.

2 Whisk the eggs, sugar and salt in a bowl. Whisk in the flour, beat until smooth and finally whisk in the milk until well combined. Melt 25 g (1 oz) of the butter and beat into the batter mixture with the apricot brandy.

3 Pour the batter over the apricots in the dish and dot with the remaining butter. Place in a preheated oven, 200°C (400°F), Gas Mark 6, for 35–40 minutes until the batter is golden and just set and the fruit is tender. Sprinkle with sugar and serve with a jug of crème fraîche.

Melon and rosewater granita

PREP
10*

COOK
5

SERVES
4–6

juicy

A fresh icy granita is perfect as a light dessert after a rich main dish, or served between courses to clear the palate. Although it takes time, it is simple to make.

1   Cut the melons in half, remove the seeds and scoop out the flesh into a food processor or blender.

2   Place the sugar and measurement water in a small saucepan and heat for about 1–2 minutes until the sugar has dissolved. Increase the heat and boil for 2 minutes without stirring, then remove the pan from heat and leave to cool slightly.

3   Add half of the sugar syrup to the melon flesh and blend until smooth. Pour it into a bowl and stir in the rosewater and more sugar syrup to taste; the amount you need will depend on the sweetness of the fruit.

4   Pour the melon mixture into a 25 x 15 cm (10 x 6 inch) tin and chill in the refrigerator. When the mixture is quite cold, transfer the tin to the freezer for 1 hour or until ice crystals have formed around the rim and the mixture is starting to freeze on the base. Stir the mixture thoroughly with a fork, then replace in the freezer. Repeat every 45 minutes until uniform crystals have formed. This will take approximately 4–5 hours. Serve at once or within 4–6 hours. To serve, spoon into glasses and top with a dollop of fromage frais, if liked.

2 **Charentais melons** or **rock melons**

75 g (3 oz) **caster sugar**

175 ml (6 fl oz) **water**

½ teaspoon **rosewater**

fromage frais, to serve (optional)

* plus 5–6 hours freezing

500 g (1 lb) cooked **chestnuts**, peeled

125 g (4 oz) **butter**, softened

200 g (7 oz) **caster sugar**

½ teaspoon **vanilla essence**

2 **eggs**, separated, plus 1 **egg white**

1 teaspoon **fennel seeds**, crushed (optional)

icing sugar, for dusting

PERSIMMON POTS

6–8 ripe **persimmons**

350 ml (12 fl oz) **double cream**

3 tablespoons **caster sugar**

grated **nutmeg**

PREP
20*

COOK
50

SERVES
6–8

creamy

Chestnut flan with persimmons

Perfect for autumn – slices of chestnut flan with puréed fruit and cream piled into frozen persimmon shells.

1 To prepare the persimmon pots, cut a 5 mm (¼ inch) slice off the top of each fruit, making a lid. Using a teaspoon, scoop the persimmon flesh into a sieve set over a bowl, leaving a thin shell. Wrap all the persimmon shells and lids in clingfilm and freeze for 1–2 hours until firm. Meanwhile, press the persimmon flesh through the sieve, discarding the stones.

2 Purée the chestnuts in a food processor or blender until smooth. Beat the butter, sugar and vanilla essence until light and fluffy. Stir in the egg yolks, chestnut purée and fennel seeds, if using, and mix well.

3 Whisk the egg whites in a grease-free bowl until stiff but not dry. Stir a quarter into the chestnut mixture to loosen it, then gently fold in the rest.

4 Spoon the mixture into a 20 cm (8 inch) fluted flan tin and level the surface. Bake in a preheated oven, 160°C (325°F), Gas Mark 3, for 40–50 minutes, until a skewer comes out clean. Cool slightly, then transfer to a wire rack to cool completely.

5 Whisk the cream with the sugar and nutmeg until it forms soft peaks. Fold in the persimmon purée, then spoon the mixture into the frozen shells and top with the lids. Dust the flan with the icing sugar and serve with the persimmon cream pots.

* plus 1–2 hours freezing

Chocolate and nut meringue stack

This recipe makes a great centrepiece and will serve up to 10 people. If you are feeling really decadent you could serve it with a hot, glossy chocolate sauce.

1 Line 4 baking sheets with nonstick baking paper. Draw a 20 cm (8 inch) circle on each one. Sift the cocoa powder and icing sugar into a small bowl. Place the egg whites and salt in a separate, grease-free bowl and whisk until stiff but not dry. Gradually whisk in the caster sugar, 1 tablespoon at a time. Fold in the icing sugar mixture and chopped pine nuts until combined.

2 Divide the meringue mixture evenly between the circles on the lined baking sheets and spread out evenly with a palette knife. Place the baking sheets in a preheated oven, 150°C (300°F), Gas Mark 2, and bake for 1–1½ hours. Remove from the oven and cool completely on wire racks.

3 To make the Marsala cream, whisk the egg yolks, caster sugar and Marsala in a bowl until creamy, then beat in the mascarpone until well combined. Place the egg whites in a separate, grease-free bowl and whisk until stiff but not dry, then fold them into the mascarpone mixture.

4 Divide the Marsala cream mixture among 3 of the meringue bases, spreading to the edges. Stack the cream-topped meringues on top of each other on a plate, then crush the last layer into small pieces and sprinkle on top. Chill for 2–4 hours, then serve lightly dusted with icing sugar and cocoa powder.

PREP
35*

COOK
90

SERVES
8–10

crisp

50 g (2 oz) **cocoa powder**

125 g (4 oz) **icing sugar**

6 **egg whites**

pinch of **salt**

175 g (6 oz) **caster sugar**

125 g (4 oz) **pine nuts**, toasted and chopped

icing sugar and **cocoa powder**, to decorate

MARSALA CREAM

2 **eggs**, separated

2 tablespoons **caster sugar**

2 tablespoons **Marsala**

500 g (1 lb) **mascarpone cheese**

* plus 2–4 hours chilling

salsas and dips

250 ml (8 fl oz) **tomato ketchup** (see page 231)

125 ml (4 fl oz) **tomato purée**

125 ml (4 fl oz) **apple cider vinegar**

4 tablespoons **blackstrap molasses**

1 tablespoon **Worcestershire sauce**

1 teaspoon **Dijon mustard**

1 teaspoon **Tabasco sauce** (or Chipotle Tabasco)

PREP
5

COOK
10

MAKES
450 ml
(¾ pint)

easy

Quick BBQ sauce

This classic sauce will go with most burgers. Chipotle Tabasco sauce, if you can find it, has a smoky yet subtle chilli flavour that works well in this recipe.

1 Place all the ingredients in a heavy-based saucepan and bring to the boil. Reduce the heat and simmer over a medium heat for 5–10 minutes or until thick.

2 Pour the sauce into sterilized jars, seal and leave to cool. Use immediately or store in the refrigerator for up to 2 weeks.

Tomato ketchup

PREP
20*

COOK
130

MAKES
600 ml
(1 pint)

classic

Making your own ketchup takes a little time, but the lack of artificial sweeteners and preservatives makes a far superior sauce – well worth the effort.

1 Place all the ingredients in a heavy saucepan and bring to the boil. Reduce the heat and simmer over a medium heat for 35 minutes, stirring frequently.

2 Remove the pan from the heat, cover and leave to stand for 1–2 hours. This will allow the flavours to blend together.

3 Push the mixture through a fine sieve, discarding the mushy skins left in the sieve. Wash out the pan and pour in the sieved tomato mixture. Bring the ketchup back to the boil and simmer it over a low heat for about 1½ hours until thick, stirring occasionally.

4 Pour the ketchup into sterilized bottles or jars, seal and leave to cool. Use immediately or store for up to 1 month in the refrigerator.

3 kg (6 lb) ripe **tomatoes**, roughly chopped

1 **onion**, chopped

1 **garlic clove**, chopped

1 **red pepper**, deseeded and chopped

250 ml (8 fl oz) **cider vinegar**

200 g (7 oz) **sugar**

1 tablespoon **green peppercorns**

1 teaspoon **salt**

1 teaspoon **English mustard powder**

½ teaspoon **ground allspice**

½ teaspoon **cayenne pepper**

¼ teaspoon **ground cloves** or 5 **whole cloves**

* plus 1–2 hours standing

15 **chillies**, deseeded and finely chopped

250 g (8 oz) **granulated sugar**

150 ml (¼ pint) **rice wine vinegar**

150 ml (¼ pint) **water**

½ teaspoon **salt**

¼ teaspoon **pepper**

juice of 1 **lemon**

Sweet chilli sauce

PREP
15

COOK
25

This Thai sauce is particularly good with Thai fish cakes and deep-fried chicken or fish.

MAKES
300 ml (½ pint)

spicy

1 Place the chillies in a saucepan with the sugar, rice vinegar and measurement water. Heat gently to dissolve the sugar, then increase the heat and simmer briskly for 20–25 minutes or until the liquid has reduced to a syrup.

2 Remove the pan from the heat and leave to cool. Add the salt, pepper and lemon juice. Pour the sauce into a sterilized container, seal and leave to cool. Use immediately or store the sauce for up to 1 month in the refrigerator.

Tomato and sweet chilli relish

Great with burgers and sausages, this classic sweet relish is a storecupboard must-have when it comes to barbecues.

1 Place the chillies, garlic and half the tomatoes in a food processor and whizz until puréed.

2 Pour the purée into a large heavy-based pan with the sugar, vinegar and remaining tomatoes. Bring to the boil, then reduce the heat and simmer for about 40–45 minutes or until thick, stirring occasionally. Set aside to cool slightly.

3 Pour the relish into sterilized jars, seal and leave to cool. Use immediately or store for up to 2 weeks in the refrigerator.

PREP
15

COOK
45

MAKES
**300 ml
(½ pint)**

sweet

5 large **red chillies**, deseeded and chopped

3 **garlic cloves**, chopped

500 g (1 lb) **tomatoes**, diced

125 g (4 oz) **sugar**

125 ml (4 fl oz) **red wine vinegar**

2 **red peppers**, deseeded and cut into quarters

1 **yellow pepper**, deseeded and cut into quarters

2 tablespoons chopped **basil**

1½ tablespoons **balsamic vinegar**

3 tablespoons **olive oil**

3 **garlic cloves**, sliced

1 teaspoon **smoked paprika**

salt and **pepper**

PREP
20

COOK
10

MAKES
**350 ml
(12 fl oz)**

smoky

Smoky pepper relish

It is the paprika that gives this relish its smoky barbecue flavour and it is particularly delicious when served with cold meat.

1 Grill the pepper quarters, skin side down, on an oiled barbecue grill over hot coals for 6–8 minutes until charred and tender. Place in a plastic bag, seal and set aside until cool enough to handle. Peel off the skin and slice the flesh into strips. Add to a bowl with the basil and balsamic vinegar.

2 Heat the oil and fry the garlic and paprika until the garlic is just starting to brown, then pour the oil over the peppers. Season with salt and pepper and mix well.

3 Spoon the relish into a sterilized jar, seal and leave to cool. Use the relish immediately or it can be stored for up to 1 week in the refrigerator.

Thousand island dressing

This classic dressing is delicious with all kinds of fish and seafood. It can be bought in most supermarkets, but the homemade version is infinitely superior.

1 Mix the mayonnaise with the paprika, onion, garlic salt and tomato purée in a bowl. Add the remaining ingredients and mix well to blend.

2 Set aside for at least 15 minutes to allow the flavours to develop before using.

PREP
10*

MAKES
**350 ml
(12 fl oz)**

classic

½ quantity **Mayonnaise** (see page 236)

½ teaspoon **paprika**

1 teaspoon grated **onion**

pinch of **garlic salt**

½ teaspoon **tomato purée**

2 teaspoons chopped **parsley**

3 tablespoons finely chopped **red pepper**

3 tablespoons finely chopped **green pepper**

2 tablespoons finely chopped **celery**

2 **green olives** or 1 small **gherkin**, finely chopped

* plus 15 minutes standing

2 large **egg yolks**

1 teaspoon **English mustard powder**

a good pinch of **salt**

1–2 tablespoons **lemon juice**

175 ml (6 fl oz) **groundnut oil**

100 ml (3½ fl oz) **extra virgin olive oil**

PREP
20

MAKES
**300 ml
(½ pint)**

classic

Mayonnaise

Making your own mayonnaise takes a bit of practice and is a little time consuming, but the difference in flavour is noticeable.

1 Whisk together the yolks, mustard, salt and lemon juice in a bowl, preferably one with a narrow base. Place the bowl on a damp cloth, to help hold it steady, so you have a free hand to pour in the oil. Alternatively, use a blender or liquidizer.

2 When the yolks are blended, start adding the oils a few drops at a time, whisking well between each addition. Once the mixture starts to thicken, you can start pouring in the oil in a very thin, steady stream. If the mayonnaise curdles, simply whisk another yolk in a clean bowl and slowly add the curdled sauce to it, whisking continuously. If you are using a blender, gradually add the oil while blending at the same time.

3 When you have added all the oil, check the mayonnaise for taste and consistency, adding lemon juice for sharpness and salt and mustard to taste. If you want a lighter consistency, whisk in 1–2 tablespoons of boiling water.

Basil mayonnaise

PREP
20

MAKES
300 ml
(½ pint)

fresh

This is an interesting twist on classic mayonnaise. If you aren't keen on the strong flavour of basil, try coriander or chives as an alternative.

1 Whisk together the yolks, mustard, salt and lemon juice in a bowl, preferably one with a narrow base. Place the bowl on a damp cloth, to help hold it steady, so you have a free hand to pour in the oil. Alternatively, use a blender or liquidizer.

2 When the yolks are blended, start adding the oils a few drops at a time, whisking well between each addition. Once the mixture starts to thicken, you can start pouring in the oil in a very thin, steady stream. If the mayonnaise curdles, simply whisk another yolk in a clean bowl and slowly add the curdled sauce to it, whisking continuously. If you are using a blender, gradually add the oil while blending at the same time.

3 When you have added all the oil, check the taste and consistency, adding lemon juice for sharpness and salt and mustard to taste. Stir the freshly chopped basil into the finished mayonnaise.

2 large **egg yolks**

1 teaspoon **English mustard powder**

a good pinch of **salt**

1–2 tablespoons **lemon juice**

175 ml (6 fl oz) **groundnut oil**

100 ml (3½ fl oz) **extra virgin olive oil**

4 tablespoons **basil**, chopped

2 large **egg yolks**

1 teaspoon **English mustard powder**

a good pinch of **salt**

1–2 tablespoons **lemon juice**

175 ml (6 fl oz) **groundnut oil**

100 ml (3½ fl oz) **extra virgin olive oil**

1 tablespoon **creamed horseradish**

PREP
20

MAKES
**300 ml
(½ pint)**

hot

Horseradish mayonnaise

The spicy hot flavour of horseradish combined with the mayonnaise is delicious served with steaks hot off the barbecue.

1 Whisk together the yolks, mustard, salt and lemon juice in a bowl, preferably one with a narrow base. Place the bowl on a damp cloth, to help hold it steady, so you have a free hand to pour in the oil. Alternatively, use a blender or liquidizer.

2 When the yolks are blended, start adding the oils a few drops at a time, whisking well between each addition. Once the mixture starts to thicken, you can start pouring in the oil in a very thin, steady stream. If the mayonnaise curdles, simply whisk another yolk in a clean bowl and slowly add the curdled sauce to it, whisking continuously. If you are using a blender, gradually add the oil while blending at the same time.

3 When you have added all the oil, check the taste and consistency, adding lemon juice for sharpness and salt and mustard to taste.

4 Stir the creamed horseradish into the finished mayonnaise.

Lemon mayonnaise

PREP
20

MAKES
300 ml
(½ pint)

fresh

A fresh, zesty alternative to classic mayonnaise – serve it with potato wedges, fish or with warm bread and a salad.

2 large **egg yolks**

1 teaspoon **English mustard powder**

a good pinch of **salt**

1–2 tablespoons **lemon juice**, plus extra to taste

175 ml (6 fl oz) **groundnut oil**

100 ml (3½ fl oz) **extra virgin olive oil**

2 tablespoons grated **lemon rind**

1 Whisk together the yolks, mustard, salt and lemon juice in a bowl, preferably one with a narrow base. Place the bowl on a damp cloth, to help hold it steady, so you have a free hand to pour in the oil. Alternatively, use a blender or liquidizer.

2 When the yolks are blended, start adding the oils a few drops at a time, whisking well between each addition. Once the mixture starts to thicken, you can start pouring in the oil in a very thin, steady stream. If the mayonnaise curdles, simply whisk another yolk in a clean bowl and slowly add the curdled sauce to it, whisking continuously. If you are using a blender, gradually add the oil while blending at the same time.

3 When you have added all the oil, check the taste and consistency, adding lemon juice for sharpness and salt and mustard to taste.

4 Stir the lemon rind into the finished mayonnaise. Add a few drops of lemon juice to lighten the mixture, if necessary.

2 large **egg yolks**

1 tablespoon **wholegrain mustard**

a good pinch of **salt**

1–2 tablespoons **lemon juice**

175 ml (6 fl oz) **groundnut oil**

100 ml (3½ fl oz) **extra virgin olive oil**

PREP
20

MAKES
300 ml
(½ pint)

tangy

Wholegrain mustard mayonnaise

Mustard and mayonnaise in one – great served with burgers, sausages or steaks in buns.

1 Whisk together the yolks, mustard, salt and lemon juice in a bowl, preferably one with a narrow base. Place the bowl on a damp cloth, to help hold it steady, so you have a free hand to pour in the oil. Alternatively, use a blender or liquidizer.

2 When the yolks are blended, start adding the oils a few drops at a time, whisking well between each addition. Once the mixture starts to thicken, you can start pouring in the oil in a very thin, steady stream. If the mayonnaise curdles, simply whisk another yolk in a clean bowl and slowly add the curdled sauce to it, whisking continuously. If you are using a blender, gradually add the oil while blending at the same time.

3 When you have added all the oil, check the taste and consistency, adding lemon juice for sharpness and salt and mustard to taste.

Aïoli or garlic mayonnaise

PREP
10*

MAKES
**300 ml
(½ pint)**

classic

Ail is the French word for garlic, hence the name Aïoli. This rich garlicky mayonnaise can be served with almost anything.

1 Crush the garlic cloves with the sea salt in a mortar or pound them together on a board with the side of a knife blade. Transfer them to a food processor with the egg yolks, lemon juice and mustard and whizz briefly until pale.

2 With the motor running, add the oil in a thin, steady stream through the feeder funnel until the sauce is emulsified, thick and glossy. You may need to thin it slightly by whisking in a spoonful or two of boiling water. Cover the surface with clingfilm and chill until required.

2–8 **garlic cloves**, according to taste

½ teaspoon **sea salt**

2 **egg yolks**

1 tablespoon **lemon juice**

1 teaspoon **Dijon mustard**

300 ml (½ pint) **extra virgin olive oil**

1–2 teaspoons boiling **water** (optional)

1 **red onion**, finely chopped

425 g (14 oz) small **vine-ripened tomatoes**, halved, deseeded and chopped

2 **garlic cloves**, crushed

15 g (½ oz) **coriander leaves**, chopped

salt and **pepper**

PREP
10*

MAKES
**350 ml
(12 fl oz)**

fresh

Coriander and tomato salsa

Serve this salsa with cold meats or as a side dish with curries and other spicy foods.

1 Put all the ingredients in a bowl and mix them together. Season lightly with salt and pepper, then cover and chill for at least 30 minutes in order for the flavours to develop.

* plus 30 minutes
chilling

Hot papaya and roasted pepper salsa

Sweet and tangy, this salsa is delicious with grilled or fried meat, chicken, fish and vegetables. It is best eaten the day it is made.

1 Combine the lime juice, olive oil and balsamic vinegar in a bowl. Add the papayas, chilli, spring onions and roasted red peppers and toss gently until combined. Season with salt and pepper and stir in the coriander.

2 Cover and chill for about 30 minutes before serving to allow the flavours to blend and develop.

PREP
15*

MAKES
**400 ml
(14 fl oz)**

tangy

juice of 1–2 **limes**

4 tablespoons light **olive oil**

¼ teaspoon **balsamic vinegar**

2 ripe **papayas**, peeled, deseeded and cut into 1 cm (½ inch) dice

½ small **red chilli**, finely chopped

2 **spring onions**, finely chopped

2 **roasted red peppers**, cored, deseeded and cut into 5 mm (¼ inch) dice

1 tablespoon finely chopped **coriander**

salt and **pepper**

* plus 30 minutes chilling

Guacamole

2 large ripe **avocados**, halved, pitted and peeled

juice of 1 **lime** or **lemon**

1 **garlic clove**, crushed

1 tablespoon finely chopped **onion**

1 large **tomato**, skinned (see page 13), deseeded and finely chopped

1–2 **green chillies**, deseeded and finely chopped

1 tablespoon finely chopped **coriander leaves**

pinch of **sugar**

salt and **pepper**

sprigs of **coriander**, to garnish

PREP
10*

MAKES
500 ml
(17 fl oz)

creamy

This thick, creamy avocado purée from Mexico can be used as a dip or as a sauce for fish and chicken.

1 Put the avocados into a bowl with the lime or lemon juice and mash with a fork to make a textured paste. Stir in the remaining ingredients, season with salt and pepper and add some extra lime or lemon juice, if required.

2 Spoon the guacamole into a serving bowl. Cover with clingfilm to help prevent discoloration and then chill until required. Serve garnished with sprigs of coriander.

* plus chilling

Chilli bean dip

PREP
15*

COOK
8

This spicy dip is excellent with crudités, corn chips or Pitta Chips (see page 201). It is also good spread on bruschetta and crostini, like a pâté.

1 Grill the pepper quarters, skin side down, on an oiled barbecue grill over hot coals for 6–8 minutes until charred and tender. Put into a plastic bag, seal and set aside until cool enough to handle. Peel off the skin and slice the flesh into strips.

2 Put the red pepper flesh, garlic and chilli in a food processor or blender until well chopped. Add the beans and paprika and continue to process until it forms a coarse purée. This won't take long. Season with Tabasco, if using, and salt and pepper. With the motor running, slowly add the oil in a thin, steady stream to make a thick paste.

3 Pile the bean purée into a bowl and sprinkle with the chopped chives. Cover and chill until required.

MAKES
**400 ml
(14 fl oz)**

fiery

2 large **red peppers**, deseeded and cut into quarters

2 **garlic cloves**, crushed

1 small **red chilli**, deseeded and finely chopped

400 g (13 oz) can **red kidney beans**, drained

½ teaspoon **paprika**

few drops of **Tabasco sauce** (optional)

salt and **pepper**

2 tablespoons **olive oil**

2 tablespoons snipped **chives**, to garnish

Hummus

400 g (13 oz) can **chickpeas**, drained and rinsed

2 **garlic cloves**, crushed

2–3 tablespoons **lemon juice**

150 ml (¼ pint) **tahini**

about 150 ml (¼ pint) **olive oil** or **sunflower oil**

2–4 tablespoons **natural set yogurt** or hot **water**

salt and **pepper**

cayenne pepper or **paprika**, to serve

PREP
10

MAKES
**300 ml
(½ pint)**

nutty

This creamy dip comes from the Middle East. It is made from chickpeas and tahini. It is easy to make at home and the results are so much nicer.

1 Put the chickpeas into a food processor or blender with the garlic, lemon juice, tahini and salt and pepper to taste. Process to a smooth paste.

2 Very gradually add the oil in a thin, steady stream. Stir in the yogurt or hot water to give the required consistency. Adjust the seasoning to taste.

3 Spoon the hummus into a serving dish, then smooth it level with the back of a spoon. To serve, pour over a little oil and dust with a sprinkling of cayenne or paprika.

Tapenade

PREP
10

MAKES
300 ml
(½ pint)

rustic

The word tapenade comes from '*tapeno*', the old Provençal word for caper, traditionally an important ingredient.

1 Pound the olives, capers, anchovies, garlic and mustard in a mortar to make a paste. Transfer it to a bowl and work in the oil a drop at a time initially, then add it a little more quickly. Mix in the thyme, lemon juice and plenty of black pepper. Taste and adjust the consistency (tapenade should be a thick, spreadable paste) and pungency if necessary, adding more oil to mellow it.

2 Tapenade can be used immediately, or you can store it for up to 3 weeks in the refrigerator.

200 g (7 oz) **black olives**, pitted

50 g (2 oz) **capers**

4 **anchovy fillets**, rinsed if necessary

1–2 **garlic cloves**, crushed

1 tablespoon **Dijon mustard**

125 ml (4 fl oz) **olive oil**

1 teaspoon crumbled **thyme**

lemon juice, to taste

pepper

200 ml (7 fl oz) **natural yogurt**

7.5 cm (3 inch) piece of **cucumber**, peeled and coarsely grated or chopped

2 tablespoons chopped **mint**

pinch of **ground cumin**

squeeze of **lemon juice** or **lime juice**

pepper

sprigs of **mint**, to garnish

PREP
10*

MAKES
**300 ml
(½ pint)**

mild

Cucumber and mint raita

A mild-flavoured and refreshing Indian yogurt dish, a perfect accompaniment to any spicy, highly seasoned meat, fish or vegetable. Chopped fresh chilli, coriander leaves or mint sauce can be added.

1 Put the yogurt in a bowl and beat lightly with a fork or whisk until smooth. Add the cucumber, mint, cumin, lemon or lime juice and pepper and stir to combine. Cover and chill until required.

2 Serve chilled, garnished with mint sprigs.

Herbed yogurt dip

Greek yogurt makes an excellent base for quick dips such as this one.

PREP
10

MAKES
**375 ml
(13 fl oz)**

simple

1 Put the basil, parsley, lemon thyme, garlic, almonds, lemon rind and olive oil in a small food processor or blender and whizz to a fine paste. Season with salt and pepper.

2 Spoon the yogurt into a serving bowl and fold the herb mixture into it, creating a marbled effect. Serve immediately.

20 g (¾ oz) **basil leaves**

15 g (½ oz) **flat leaf parsley**

15 g (½ oz) **lemon thyme**

1 **garlic clove**, peeled

25 g (1 oz) **toasted almonds**

grated rind of 1 **lemon**

5 tablespoons **olive oil**

250 g (8 oz) **Greek yogurt**

salt and **pepper**

4 tablespoons **olive oil**

4 **garlic cloves**, crushed

125 ml (4 fl oz) **dry white wine**

1 small **onion**, finely chopped

1 sprig each of **rosemary, thyme** and **parsley**

Herb marinade

PREP 5

SERVES 4

A simple marinade that will work equally well with meat and fish.

tasty

1 Mix together all the ingredients and pour them over the fish or meat in a shallow, non-metallic dish.

2 Cover and leave to marinate in the refrigerator for several hours or overnight.

125 ml (4 fl oz) **hoisin sauce**

3 tablespoons **tomato purée**

2 tablespoons **lemon juice**

2 tablespoons **honey**

2 tablespoons **soy sauce**

Hoisin marinade

PREP 5

SERVES 4

This marinade is rich and sweet, so use it sparingly. It is a particularly good marinade for spare ribs or chops.

oriental

1 Mix together all the ingredients and pour them over the fish, chicken or meat in a shallow, non-metallic dish.

2 Cover the dish and leave to marinate for at least 30 minutes.

Sweet and sour marinade

PREP 5

SERVES 4

classic

A classic bittersweet Chinese marinade – perfect with fish or chicken.

4 tablespoons **tomato ketchup**

2 tablespoons **Worcestershire sauce**

2 tablespoons **white wine vinegar**

2 tablespoons **honey**

2 tablespoons **soft brown sugar**

1 Mix together all the ingredients and pour over the fish or chicken in a shallow, non-metallic dish.

2 Cover and leave to marinate in the refrigerator for several hours or overnight.

Barbecue marinade

PREP 5

SERVES 6

sticky

The classic barbecue marinade, no barbecue would be complete without it. Add more chilli powder, to taste, for a spicier version.

1 teaspoon **mustard powder**

1 teaspoon **salt**

½ teaspoon **chilli powder**

1 tablespoon **dark brown sugar**

300 g (10 oz) can **condensed tomato soup**

2 tablespoons **vinegar**

2 tablespoons **Worcestershire sauce**

2 tablespoons **soy sauce**

1 Mix together all the ingredients and pour them over the meat in a shallow, non-metallic dish.

2 Cover and leave to marinate in a cool place for at least 1–2 hours.

index

acknowledgements

Executive Editor Nicola Hill
Managing Editor Clare Churly
Design Manager Tokiko Morishima
Designer Ginny Zeal
Illustrator Sudden Impact Media
Senior Production Controller Manjit Sihra